I0782899

Trivia Mania

A Random Collection of Fun Facts and Trivia Gems

Trivia Mania
A Random Collection of Fun Facts and Trivia Gems

While every effort has been made to ensure the accuracy of the facts presented, remember that the universe is a weird and ever-evolving place. New discoveries might someday prove that some of these nuggets of knowledge are a little less golden than we thought. (Science and history are tricky like that.) If you're ever questioned about a particularly odd fact, just smile knowingly and say, "I read it in a trivia book. Trust me, it's legit."

Also, we accept no responsibility for any friendships strained, family members baffled, or debates sparked by your newfound trivia prowess. Use this information responsibly — unless you're trying to one-up your overly confident cousin during Thanksgiving. Then, by all means, go for it.

Finally, remember: this book is for fun, entertainment, and the joy of learning something new. If you laugh, gasp, or have a *Wait, What!* moment while reading, we've done our job. Now, go forth and trivia on!

ISBN: 9798303163331
Independently Published

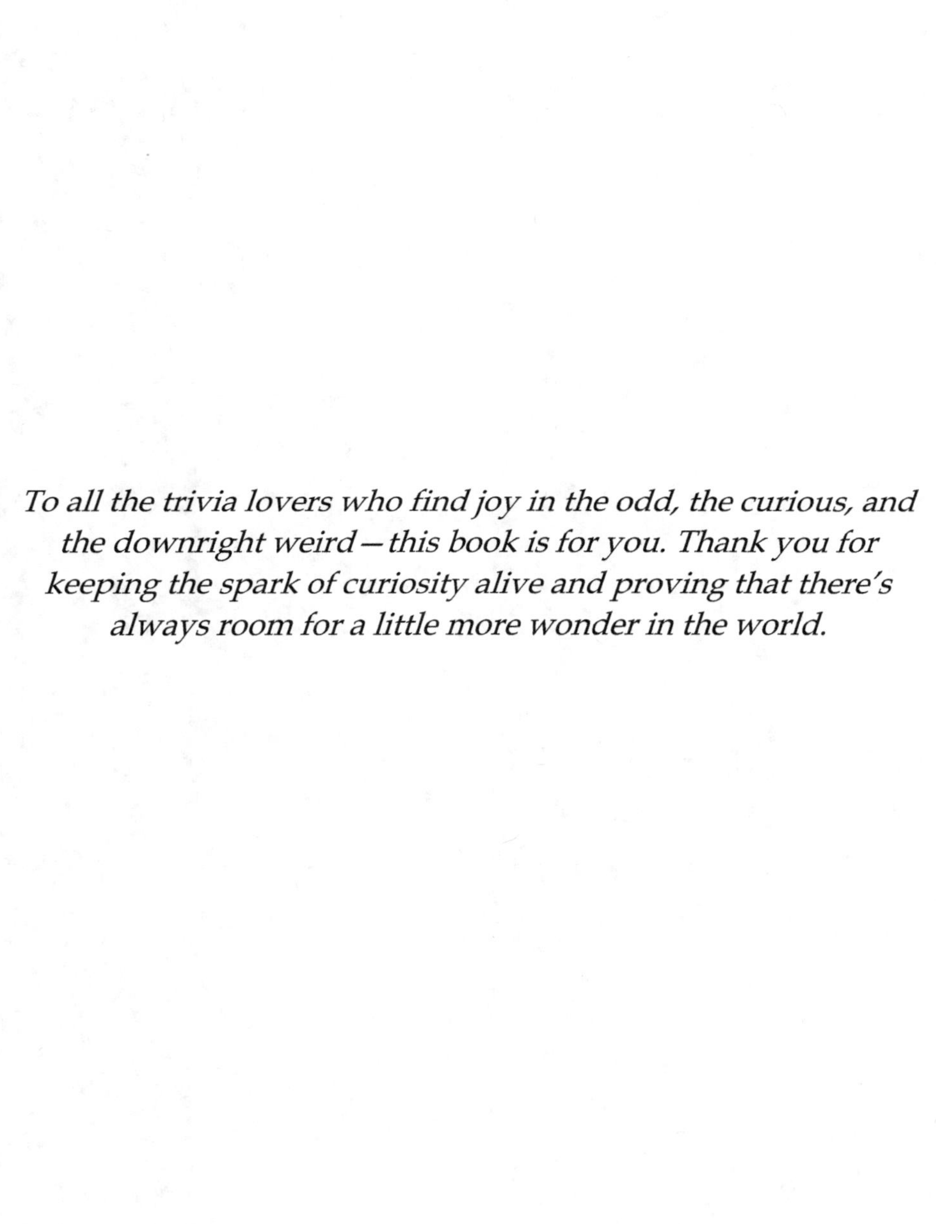

To all the trivia lovers who find joy in the odd, the curious, and the downright weird—this book is for you. Thank you for keeping the spark of curiosity alive and proving that there's always room for a little more wonder in the world.

Table of Contents

Random Trivia Fun   9

Environmental Mysteries   11

Biological Oddities   27

Sociological Marvels   43

Psychological Phenomena   57

Economic Peculiarities   71

Medical Madness   83

Astronomical Oddities   95

Technological Marvels   107

Geological Curiosities   119

Fun Quiz: Your Trivia Buffness   135

Random Trivia Fun

Have you ever been the person who drops a bizarre fact into a conversation and watches as everyone's eyes light up with amazement—or confusion? Do you take a certain delight in knowing things like why flamingos are pink or that Saturn has a six-sided storm at its north pole?

If so, congratulations! You're in the right place.

If not, don't worry—by the end of this book, you'll be armed with an arsenal of delightful, mind-bending trivia to impress your friends, stump your family, and perhaps even win a pub quiz or two.

This book isn't just about random facts; it's about rediscovering the joy of curiosity. We live in a world bursting with oddities, marvels, and downright strange phenomena, many of which are hidden in plain sight. Every fact here is a tiny adventure—a peek into the extraordinary details of life, the universe, and everything in between. Think of this book as your ticket to becoming a modern-day explorer, delving into the nooks and crannies of knowledge that often go overlooked.

Learning trivia isn't just fun—it's powerful. Knowing something unexpected sparks conversations, builds connections, and, let's be honest, gives you a fantastic edge in any awkward small-talk situation. Who needs weather chat when you can casually mention the planet that rains glass sideways or the discovery of a 10-billion-trillion-carat diamond star? With these little nuggets of knowledge, you'll become the life of every gathering — or at least the most intriguing person in the room.

But beyond impressing others, trivia is also about rekindling your sense of wonder. There's something magical about stumbling upon a fact so strange, so unbelievable, that it stops you in your tracks. You pause, smile, and think, How is that even possible? That moment of awe is what this book is all about. Whether it's uncovering the secrets of zombie stars, exploring the traditions of distant cultures, or marveling at the quirks of our own biology, these pages are packed with moments designed to make you think, laugh, and marvel.

Of course, this book isn't a test. There are no pop quizzes or grades here — only the joy of learning for its own sake. Flip through at your leisure. Pick a chapter that piques your interest or dive straight into the randomness of it all. Whether you're a science buff, a history nerd, or someone who just enjoys a good story, there's something here for everyone.

So, what can you expect? Tales of nature's oddities, the wonders of space, the mysteries of history, and the quirks of human behavior, all told with a blend of curiosity and humor. From the depths of the ocean to the farthest reaches of the galaxy, this book is a celebration of the strange and the extraordinary.

So grab a comfy chair, a curious mind, and perhaps a cup of tea (or a trivia-loving friend). You're about to embark on a journey through the unexpected, the baffling, and the downright entertaining. And who knows? By the time you're done, you might just be the one who leaves everyone else thinking, *Wow, I didn't know that!*

Environmental Mysteries

The Taos Hum

If you've ever had an annoying song stuck in your head, imagine if instead of a tune, it was a low, constant hum that followed you everywhere.

That's life for some residents of Taos, New Mexico.

This peculiar noise, dubbed the "Taos Hum," is a persistent low-frequency sound that not everyone can hear. While estimates vary, around 2% of Taos locals report hearing this enigmatic buzz, often likened to the drone of distant machinery or a swarm of bees.

But here's the kicker: no one has ever definitively found its source. Scientists, conspiracy theorists, and amateur sleuths alike have tried to pin it on everything from underground seismic activity to secret government experiments (because what unsolved mystery doesn't involve the government?). Some suggest it's a form of tinnitus, while others claim it's a global phenomenon, with similar hums reported in places like Bristol, England, and Largs, Scotland. The hum's elusiveness only deepens the intrigue; sound equipment often fails to detect it.

Is it an auditory illusion? A sign of impending alien contact? Whatever the cause, the Taos Hum remains one of Earth's strangest unsolved riddles. Meanwhile, the unlucky few who hear it are stuck searching for peace and quiet while the rest of us marvel at their buzzing plight.

The Bermuda Triangle's Environmental Oddities

The Bermuda Triangle, a mysterious swath of the Atlantic bounded by Miami, Bermuda, and Puerto Rico, has inspired more conspiracy theories than an Area 51 convention.

Ships and planes have allegedly vanished without a trace, and theories about why range from alien abductions to time warps. But while Hollywood loves a good extraterrestrial angle, science offers more grounded explanations—literally. One theory suggests the triangle's infamous disappearances may be linked to methane hydrate eruptions. When massive methane deposits trapped under the seafloor suddenly burst free, they can create explosive bubbles that reduce water density, causing ships to sink faster than you can say "Mayday!"

Then there are the magnetic anomalies. Compass readings within the triangle have been reported to go haywire, confusing navigators and sending pilots and captains off course. This may be due to magnetic fluctuations near true north. And while these explanations may not involve little green men, they still provide enough intrigue to keep the Bermuda Triangle firmly lodged in the annals of weird geography.

Whether you believe in alien abductions or methane burps, there's no denying that this enigmatic area keeps our imagination—and compasses—spinning.

The Disappearing Aral Sea

Once upon a time, the Aral Sea was a shimmering blue jewel straddling Kazakhstan and Uzbekistan, known as the fourth-largest lake in the world. Today, it's a desolate wasteland, a ghost of its former self.

What happened?

In a tragic example of human interference gone awry, the Soviet Union decided to divert the rivers feeding the Aral Sea to irrigate cotton fields. By the 1980s, water levels had plummeted, leaving behind vast stretches of salty desert and stranded fishing boats, now rusting in the sun. To add insult to ecological injury, the exposed lakebed released toxic dust from agricultural chemicals, causing respiratory problems for local populations.

The region's once-thriving fishing industry collapsed, and native species disappeared. Efforts to restore the sea have had mixed success; while Kazakhstan has seen minor improvements in the northern Aral, the southern portion remains a cautionary tale of environmental mismanagement. The Aral Sea's tragic transformation is a stark reminder that when humans mess with nature's plumbing, the consequences can be both unexpected and devastating.

The Vanishing Honeybee Population

Bees: they're not just about honey and painful stingers; they're vital to human survival.

These industrious insects pollinate about 75% of the crops we eat, making their sudden disappearance a global emergency. Colony Collapse Disorder (CCD) has baffled scientists for years. In affected colonies, worker bees abandon the hive, leaving behind a queen, a handful of nurse bees, and a lot of unanswered questions.

Possible culprits include pesticides, habitat loss, climate change, and invasive species like the aptly named "murder hornets." But the most compelling theory is neonicotinoids, a class of pesticides that seem to scramble bees' navigation systems, leaving them unable to find their way home. Without bees, entire ecosystems could unravel, leading to what experts have ominously dubbed "pollination Armageddon."

While efforts to curb pesticide use and plant bee-friendly flowers have shown promise, the mystery of CCD reminds us just how fragile our buzzing buddies — and our food supply — really are. Next time you see a bee, give it a mental high-five; it's working overtime to keep you alive.

The Mystery of Fairy Circles in Namibia

Picture the Namib Desert, one of the driest and oldest deserts in the world. Its vast, dusty expanse stretches as far as the eye can see, dotted with thousands of peculiar circular patches of barren land, each surrounded by a lush ring of vegetation. These are the "fairy circles," nature's way of telling us, "Good luck figuring me out." Locals whisper that these circles are the footprints of gods or the playful handiwork of spirits. It's hard not to see why; their near-perfect geometry and enigmatic origins feel otherworldly.

Scientists, on the other hand, have tried to play the buzzkill, coming up with rational theories. Some say it's the work of termites, those tiny construction workers of the desert, munching away at plant roots and creating barren centers where moisture collects, letting the surrounding grasses thrive. Others argue it's not termites at all but plants fighting for survival. In the desert, water is life, and plants supposedly collaborate to space themselves just right, ensuring everyone gets a fair share of moisture. Cooperative plants? That almost sounds like science fiction.

Despite decades of research, the jury is still out. In the meantime, the fairy circles continue to grow, shrink, and mysteriously vanish, teasing scientists and delighting tourists. Whatever their cause, they remain a captivating reminder that nature has a flair for the mysterious—and that sometimes, the simplest places hold the most complex puzzles.

The Sargasso Sea's Floating Forest

Welcome to the Sargasso Sea, a stretch of ocean with no borders. This isn't your average body of water—it's defined not by coastlines but by swirling currents that corral massive mats of sargassum seaweed into one of the most peculiar ecosystems on the planet. These floating golden-green carpets form a home for countless creatures, from baby sea turtles hitching a ride to camouflaged crabs playing hide-and-seek.

Sailors of old found the Sargasso Sea both fascinating and terrifying. Tales of ghost ships adrift in the dense weed only added to its mystique. In reality, the seaweed poses no real threat to vessels; the swirling gyres of current are a greater challenge. These same currents, however, are what make the Sargasso Sea unique, concentrating nutrients and creating a marine paradise. For fish, shrimp, and even migratory eels, it's an underwater buffet.

Modern science has revealed that the Sargasso Sea is not just a haven for marine life but also a vital carbon sink. The seaweed absorbs CO2, helping mitigate climate change. Unfortunately, this floating forest isn't immune to human impact. Plastic pollution often collects here alongside the seaweed, turning parts of this natural wonder into a cautionary tale of our environmental footprint. Still, the Sargasso Sea remains a marvel—a borderless world that thrives on the fringes of chaos and calm.

The Baltic Sea Anomaly

In 2011, a team of Swedish treasure hunters stumbled upon something truly bizarre at the bottom of the Baltic Sea. What they found wasn't gold or sunken ships but an object that looked eerily like the Millennium Falcon from Star Wars. Naturally, the world's collective imagination ran wild. Was it an alien spacecraft? A secret Nazi weapon? Or just a particularly cool rock formation?

The anomaly, sitting 300 feet below the surface, is about 200 feet wide with features that resemble ramps, staircases, and even scorch marks. Sonar images fueled conspiracy theories faster than you can say "Area 51." Scientists, however, are a less excitable bunch. Geologists suggest it could be a natural glacial deposit formed during the Ice Age. Not as fun as aliens, but probably more plausible.

Despite extensive investigations, no one has definitively explained the anomaly's origins. The lack of funding and the Baltic's murky waters haven't helped matters. For now, the object remains an underwater mystery, sparking debates, documentaries, and heated Reddit threads. Whether it's an extraterrestrial relic or just a misunderstood hunk of rock, the Baltic Sea Anomaly proves that even our planet's watery depths have stories to tell.

The Moaning Earth Phenomenon

Imagine sitting in your cozy home when the ground beneath you starts emitting an eerie, low-frequency groan. No, it's not the prelude to an earthquake or the soundtrack of a horror film—it's the Moaning Earth Phenomenon. Around the world, people have reported hearing these unexplainable sounds, often described as metallic groans, hums, or even trumpets from the heavens. Creepy? Absolutely.

Theories abound, ranging from seismic activity to atmospheric pressure shifts. Some scientists suggest these sounds could be related to tectonic plates grinding against each other, creating vibrations that travel through the Earth. Others point to natural gas escaping from underground pockets, creating noises that sound like Earth itself is exhaling. Of course, conspiracy theorists have their own ideas, involving everything from secret government experiments to, you guessed it, alien activity.

What makes the Moaning Earth so unsettling is its unpredictability. The sounds can last minutes or hours and often leave no tangible evidence. For residents in places like Windsor, Canada, or Taos, New Mexico—both infamous for strange hums—it's an everyday reminder that Earth is as mysterious as it is noisy. While scientists continue to investigate, the rest of us can't help but wonder: is the planet trying to tell us something, or is it just having a bad day?

The Blood Rain of Kerala, India

Imagine waking up one morning to find the skies weeping red.

In 2001, that's exactly what happened in Kerala, India, where rain poured down in shades of crimson, leaving locals bewildered and a little unnerved. Was it an omen? A curse? A cosmic accident?

As buckets of blood-hued water drenched the region, theories ranged from alien spores to terrestrial fungi. Scientists sampled the rain and found it contained microscopic particles, which some suggested were spores from local lichen. Yet, the story doesn't end there. A few bold researchers speculated that these particles could be extraterrestrial, arriving via a comet's dusty tail.

While the fungal theory remains the most plausible, the idea of alien biology falling to Earth gives this phenomenon a sci-fi edge. Whether celestial or Earth-born, the blood rain of Kerala remains a hauntingly beautiful mystery, a reminder that even rain can surprise us.

The Great Dying: Earth's Largest Extinction Event

Long before dinosaurs had their dramatic asteroid finale, Earth faced the ultimate "reset button" during the Permian-Triassic extinction event, also called The Great Dying.

Around 252 million years ago, this catastrophic event wiped out nearly all marine life and most terrestrial species. The oceans turned acidic, temperatures soared, and life as it was simply collapsed. The prime suspect? Gigantic volcanic eruptions in Siberia that released enough toxic gas to create a runaway greenhouse effect. But the mystery deepens with theories of asteroid impacts and methane explosions from ocean floors also vying for blame.

Whatever caused it, The Great Dying reshaped evolution itself, paving the way for dinosaurs to dominate and, eventually, humans to emerge. It's an extinction story so apocalyptic, it makes today's climate challenges look like minor inconveniences.

The Eternal Flame Falls

Nestled in New York's Shale Creek Preserve, Eternal Flame Falls is a natural oddity that blends fire and water in perfect, mind-boggling harmony.

Behind the cascading water of this small waterfall burns a flickering flame, fueled by natural methane gas seeping from beneath the ground. The flame is relatively small but stubborn, with only occasional human intervention needed to relight it when strong winds or heavy rains snuff it out. Local legends credit the flame to magical forces, but science has the less romantic explanation of naturally occurring gas leaks.

Still, the juxtaposition of fire and water feels magical, like something plucked from fantasy lore. Eternal Flame Falls is a rare geological gem, a place where opposites not only coexist but create a spectacle that continues to mesmerize visitors and defy nature's usual rules.

The Northern Migration of Magnetic North

It sounds like the plot of a disaster movie: Earth's magnetic north pole is on the move, and it's speeding up.

Once relatively stable, magnetic north has recently started migrating toward Siberia at an accelerated rate, throwing compasses—and scientists—off balance. The magnetic field, generated by swirling molten iron in Earth's outer core, isn't static, but its current movement is unusually rapid. Why? That's still a mystery, though shifts in the liquid core's dynamics are a prime suspect. While this doesn't mean GPS devices will suddenly fail, it does require regular updates to navigation systems and world maps.

And for migratory animals like birds and sea turtles, which rely on magnetic cues, this might be like having their favorite landmarks move overnight. Whether it's a prelude to a geomagnetic reversal—where north and south poles swap places—or just another quirk of our restless planet, the northern migration of magnetic north reminds us that even Earth's most reliable features can surprise us.

Lake Nyos' Killer Cloud

On a tranquil evening in 1986, Cameroon's Lake Nyos unleashed a horror straight out of a disaster novel. Without warning, a dense cloud of carbon dioxide erupted from its depths, silently suffocating over 1,700 people and countless animals. Imagine a deadly fog that creeps in and smothers everything it touches—it's not just terrifying, it's real. The culprit? Nature's own chemistry experiment gone wrong.

Lake Nyos sits atop a dormant volcano, and over centuries, volcanic activity seeped carbon dioxide into the water below. Normally, this gas remains dissolved under the pressure of the lake's depth, but on that fateful night, something—a landslide, perhaps—triggered the release. The lake became a shaken soda can, its gas exploding into the atmosphere in an invisible, lethal plume. Since carbon dioxide is heavier than air, it hugged the ground, moving silently through villages, asphyxiating everything in its path.

Today, engineers have installed pipes to safely vent the gas, turning Lake Nyos into a less volatile neighbor. Still, the memory of that night lingers—a grim reminder that even the most peaceful-looking bodies of water can hold deadly secrets. If nothing else, it proves that Mother Nature has a dark sense of humor, capable of turning serene lakes into death traps overnight.

The Underwater Forest of Alabama

Beneath the Gulf of Mexico lies an ancient wonder—a 60,000-year-old forest of bald cypress trees, preserved in eerie perfection. Unveiled after Hurricane Ivan churned the seafloor in 2004, this submerged relic feels like something from a prehistoric time capsule. The trees, entombed in sediment for millennia, were shielded from decay by the oxygen-deprived environment. Now exposed, they stand as ghostly sentinels, offering divers a chance to swim through history.

These trees once thrived on land, their roots deep in soil when the Ice Age ruled. But as glaciers melted and sea levels rose, the forest was submerged and forgotten, only to reemerge tens of thousands of years later as a hidden treasure. For marine life, it's a thriving habitat; for scientists, it's a natural laboratory, preserving clues about ancient ecosystems and climate conditions.

But this wonder is fleeting. Marine organisms are rapidly consuming the wood, turning this time capsule into an ecological buffet. Efforts to study and preserve the site are racing against the clock, as each passing year brings the loss of more of this underwater marvel. For now, the underwater forest is a hauntingly beautiful reminder that even in destruction — like a hurricane — nature reveals its timeless wonders.

The Frozen Methane Bubbles of Canada

In Alberta's Lake Abraham, winter brings a natural art installation that defies imagination. Frozen beneath the lake's icy surface are thousands of pristine white bubbles, trapped in crystal-clear layers of ice like nature's own snow globe. But these bubbles are not just pretty — they're also a potent reminder of what lurks beneath.

The bubbles form when methane gas, produced by decaying organic material at the lakebed, rises toward the surface. As the water freezes, the gas gets trapped, creating striking patterns of suspended spheres. Photographers flock to this spectacle, risking frozen fingers to capture the surreal beauty. But there's a catch — when the ice melts, the methane escapes into the atmosphere, contributing to climate change. This potent greenhouse gas is about 25 times more effective at trapping heat than carbon dioxide.

While the frozen bubbles are an undeniable visual delight, they carry an ominous message about the fragility of our planet's ecosystems. For now, visitors marvel at the sight, snapping pictures and pretending not to notice the environmental undertones. It's a curious mix of awe and unease—a stunning reminder that even the most beautiful phenomena can come with a hidden cost.

The Missing Sea of Chiquimulilla, Guatemala

One morning, residents of Chiquimulilla, Guatemala, woke up to a surreal sight: the sea was gone. Where waves once lapped, a dry, cracked basin stretched as far as the eye could see. This was no ordinary low tide—it was as if the ocean had simply packed up and left. For locals, it was a source of awe and terror, sparking fears of apocalyptic events or supernatural forces.

The reality, while less mystical, was equally dramatic. Sudden tectonic shifts beneath the Earth's crust had caused the sea to drain overnight, a rare and spectacular event tied to seismic activity. The water likely flowed into underground fissures, leaving behind an empty landscape that resembled a forgotten desert. While scientists rushed to study the phenomenon, locals were left grappling with the eerie transformation of their coastline.

For days, the empty sea basin drew visitors, who marveled at its desolation. But like all good mysteries, this one didn't last forever. The sea eventually returned, its ebb and flow as if nothing had happened. Yet the event remains etched in local lore, a strange chapter in the Earth's unpredictable story. It's a powerful reminder that even something as vast and eternal-seeming as the ocean can vanish in the blink of an eye, leaving us all humbled by nature's capricious power.

The Crooked Forest in Poland

Deep in the woods of Poland lies a grove of pine trees straight out of a fantasy novel—or a Tim Burton movie. Known as the Crooked Forest, these 400 or so trees start off growing normally, but then, a few feet off the ground, their trunks bend into a dramatic curve before straightening out again. The result is a surreal landscape of arching pines that seem to defy nature's logic. Theories about their peculiar shapes abound, from heavy snow bending the saplings to human intervention.

One popular idea is that these trees were deliberately bent by farmers in the 1930s who wanted curved wood for furniture or boat building. However, World War II disrupted their plans, and the forest was left to grow into its peculiar shape. Others speculate environmental factors—perhaps a strange combination of snow, wind, or soil conditions caused this odd growth. Still, no one knows for sure, and that's part of the allure.

Today, the Crooked Forest is a tourist hotspot, inviting visitors to wander among its strange and silent sentinels. Whether it's a quirky natural phenomenon or the result of forgotten human ingenuity, it's a place that sparks the imagination. After all, when nature throws us a curve—literally—it's hard not to stop and wonder why.

The Lake That Turns Animals to Stone

In the heart of Tanzania lies Lake Natron, a body of water so alkaline it could moonlight as a potion ingredient in a witch's brew. At first glance, its surface appears calm and inviting, but any creature unlucky enough to enter may find itself immortalized in stone—well, sort of. The lake's high pH, caused by mineral deposits from surrounding volcanic rocks, can preserve animals in eerie lifelike poses.

The lake's temperature can soar to 140°F, making it inhospitable to most forms of life. Flamingos, oddly enough, seem to thrive here, using the lake as a nesting ground. But for others, it's a death trap. When small birds or bats fall into the water, the intense alkalinity calcifies their bodies, leaving behind macabre statues. Photographer Nick Brandt captured haunting images of these calcified creatures, further cementing Lake Natron's reputation as both a natural wonder and a place to avoid swimming.

Despite its deadly reputation, the lake is vital to the ecosystem. It supports algae, which feed flamingos, and provides a stark reminder of nature's extremes. Lake Natron isn't a place for beach vacations, but it's a breathtaking testament to the power and peculiarity of Earth's natural processes.

The Silent Migration of Sea Turtles

Sea turtles might just be nature's quietest overachievers. Every year, these ancient mariners embark on epic journeys, traveling thousands of miles across oceans to return to the exact beaches where they were born. How they do this without GPS—or complaining about gas prices—remains one of nature's great mysteries.

Scientists believe sea turtles rely on the Earth's magnetic field to navigate, essentially using it as an internal compass. This "magnetic map" allows them to pinpoint their birthplace with astonishing accuracy, even decades after hatching. It's like a homing instinct on steroids. Once they reach their sandy origins, females lay their eggs in carefully dug nests before returning to the sea, leaving the next generation to figure out life on its own.

But it's not all smooth sailing for these ancient travelers. Pollution, fishing nets, and climate change threaten their survival, turning their migratory marathon into an obstacle course. Conservation efforts, including protected nesting sites and turtle-friendly fishing gear, aim to ensure these majestic creatures continue their silent journeys for generations to come. Sea turtles are proof that sometimes, the quietest travelers leave the biggest impact.

The Amazon's Dark Water Rivers

Winding through the Amazon rainforest are rivers so dark and mysterious, they look like liquid tea spilled by some clumsy giant. These "blackwater" rivers, such as the Rio Negro, get their inky hue from tannins released by decaying plant material in the surrounding forests. Don't worry, the water isn't dirty— it's just nature's way of brewing an ecosystem.

Despite their brooding appearance, these rivers are teeming with life. Fish, amphibians, and countless other species thrive in the unique chemistry of blackwater ecosystems. The rivers also play a critical role in maintaining the balance of the rainforest, transporting nutrients and serving as highways for the diverse creatures that call the Amazon home.

However, the dark waters have their own secrets. Locals often tell tales of mysterious creatures lurking below the surface, from massive anacondas to mythical beasts. While science hasn't confirmed the existence of monsters, the rivers' depths are still largely unexplored, adding to their mystique. For now, the Amazon's blackwater rivers remain a perfect blend of beauty, mystery, and ecological importance—a true testament to the rainforest's untamed spirit.

Biological Oddities

The Immortal Jellyfish

If there's one creature on Earth that could moonlight as a Marvel superhero, it's the immortal jellyfish, Turritopsis dohrnii. Native to the Mediterranean and parts of Japan, this tiny, translucent marvel has cracked the code of biological immortality. When faced with stress, injury, or the indignities of old age, it doesn't die like the rest of us mere mortals. Instead, it reverts its cells to an earlier stage of life, essentially transforming itself back into a baby jellyfish — or polyp.

This "Benjamin Button" of the ocean achieves its immortality through a process called transdifferentiation, where adult cells transform into a completely new type of cell. Think of it as nature's ultimate do-over. Of course, immortality doesn't mean invincibility; the jellyfish can still be eaten by predators or fall victim to disease. But barring bad luck, it could theoretically keep resetting itself indefinitely.

Despite its potential as a symbol of eternal youth, the immortal jellyfish is surprisingly unassuming, measuring just a few millimeters across. Its humble existence serves as a reminder that the secrets to life's greatest mysteries might be hidden in the most unexpected places — like a tiny blob floating in the sea. Scientists are studying it closely, hoping to uncover insights into aging and regenerative medicine. After all, who wouldn't want a reset button for life?

Axolotls: The Regeneration Masters

Meet the axolotl, a creature so fantastical it seems like it was dreamed up in a Pixar studio. Native to Mexico, this aquatic salamander has an uncanny ability to regenerate just about anything. Lost a limb? No problem—it'll grow back. Damaged its heart or spinal cord? It'll fix those too. In fact, axolotls can even regrow parts of their brains, making them the ultimate DIY repair experts of the animal kingdom.

What's even more impressive is how perfectly the axolotl regenerates. Unlike a lizard's tail, which might grow back a bit off-kilter, an axolotl's replacement parts are indistinguishable from the originals. Scientists are fascinated by this salamander's regenerative superpowers, studying it in hopes of unlocking medical breakthroughs for humans. Imagine healing spinal injuries or regrowing organs the way axolotls do—it's science fiction knocking on reality's door.

Despite their talents, axolotls are critically endangered in the wild, victims of habitat loss and pollution. Thankfully, they're thriving in captivity, where their perpetual "smile" and endearing gills make them popular pets. If any creature could make a case for why we should protect biodiversity, it's this plucky salamander with a knack for second chances.

The Zombie Ant Fungus

If horror movies ever needed inspiration, the zombie ant fungus would be a natural muse. This mind-controlling parasite, Ophiocordyceps unilateralis, turns ants into unwitting pawns in its sinister life cycle. The fungus infects an ant, takes over its nervous system, and compels it to climb vegetation. Once the ant is in prime spore-dispersal territory, the fungus kills its host and erupts from its body, releasing spores to infect more ants.

The precision of this macabre process is chilling. The infected ant's movements are no longer its own; the fungus manipulates it with a puppet-master's finesse. Scientists still don't fully understand how the fungus hijacks the ant's brain, but they suspect it releases chemicals that alter the ant's behavior.

While this might sound like the stuff of nightmares, the zombie ant fungus plays an essential role in ecosystems by keeping ant populations in check. It's a fascinating, albeit creepy, reminder that nature operates on a level of complexity that often defies our comprehension. For the ants, it's a grim fate; for us, it's a window into the strange and brutal ingenuity of evolution.

The Naked Mole Rat's Pain-Free Life

The naked mole rat is the underdog of the animal kingdom—literally. These wrinkly, buck-toothed rodents spend their lives burrowing underground in East Africa, where they've evolved some truly bizarre traits. For starters, they're virtually immune to pain. Thanks to unique molecular adaptations, they don't feel the burning sting of acidic environments, which would send most creatures running for cover.

Their quirks don't stop there. Naked mole rats are highly resistant to cancer, a trait that has scientists buzzing. They produce a sugary substance called hyaluronan that prevents their cells from clumping together into tumors. Combine that with their ability to survive in low-oxygen conditions that would kill most mammals, and you've got one of nature's strangest success stories.

Despite their peculiar appearance, naked mole rats are social creatures that live in colonies led by a queen. Their cooperative lifestyle resembles that of bees or ants, making them a biological anomaly among mammals. While they won't win any beauty contests, naked mole rats are proof that nature values function over form—and sometimes, being weird is a survival superpower.

The Blue Blood of Horseshoe Crabs

Horseshoe crabs may not win any beauty contests, but their unusual blood has been a lifesaver—literally. Unlike humans, whose blood gets its red hue from iron, horseshoe crabs boast copper-based blood that shines a vivid blue. But it's not just the color that makes their blood special; it contains a compound called Limulus Amebocyte Lysate (LAL), which clots in the presence of bacterial toxins. This property is so effective that LAL is used to test the safety of vaccines, IV drugs, and medical equipment, ensuring they're free from contamination.

These living fossils—unchanged for over 450 million years—are the unsung heroes of modern medicine. Every year, thousands of horseshoe crabs are "donated" for their blood in a process that's oddly reminiscent of human blood donation, though significantly less comfortable for the crab. Fortunately, most are returned to the wild afterward.

While their role in medicine is invaluable, conservationists warn of declining populations due to habitat loss and overharvesting. Researchers are working on synthetic alternatives to LAL to reduce dependence on these ancient creatures, but for now, the blue blood of horseshoe crabs remains a vital component of healthcare. It's a quirky reminder that sometimes, the most bizarre creatures play the biggest roles in saving lives.

The Immortal Clam: Ming the Mollusk

Meet Ming the Mollusk, a clam so old it was alive when the Ming Dynasty ruled China. Discovered off the coast of Iceland, this ocean-dwelling time capsule lived to the ripe old age of 507 years before scientists—ironically—accidentally killed it while studying its age. Talk about a tragic end to an epic life story.

Ming belonged to the species Arctica islandica, known for its extreme longevity. These clams grow slowly and lead uneventful lives buried in the seabed, which likely contributes to their impressive lifespans. By counting the growth rings on Ming's shell (similar to tree rings), researchers determined it was born around 1499, making it one of the longest-living non-colonial animals ever recorded.

Beyond its sheer age, Ming offers valuable insights into aging and climate history. Its shell contains chemical records of environmental changes over centuries, making it a treasure trove of data. While Ming's fate is a reminder to tread carefully with ancient creatures, its legacy lives on as a symbol of the ocean's hidden wonders—and the occasional price of curiosity.

The Deep-Sea Fish with a Transparent Head

If the deep sea needed a mascot for "weird but fascinating," the barreleye fish would be a top contender. This peculiar fish, found lurking thousands of feet below the surface, boasts a transparent head that looks more like a sci-fi prop than a real animal. Through its dome-like skull, you can see its upward-facing, tubular eyes—an adaptation that helps it spot prey in the pitch-black depths.

The barreleye's eyes are encased in a fluid-filled shield, allowing them to swivel and track faint bioluminescent light sources. If its head weren't strange enough, the fish also has nostrils above its mouth that look suspiciously like misplaced eyes. This unique anatomy has confused scientists for years, but it's perfectly suited for its dark, quiet world.

Though rare and elusive, the barreleye highlights the strange beauty of evolution's creativity. It's a reminder that the deep sea is a realm of endless surprises, where creatures adapt in ways that seem almost magical. For the barreleye, its glassy head isn't just a cool party trick—it's a survival strategy.

Glass Frogs and Their See-Through Skin

If you've ever wanted x-ray vision, look no further than the glass frog. Native to Central and South America, these tiny amphibians have translucent bellies that reveal their inner workings in astonishing detail. With their organs on full display, glass frogs seem like nature's way of showing off its handiwork, offering a rare glimpse into the anatomy of a living creature.

Why would an animal evolve such see-through skin? Scientists believe it's a form of camouflage. When perched on a leaf, the frog's translucent belly helps it blend into the dappled light of its surroundings, making it harder for predators to spot. Some species even have bones that glow under UV light, adding to their otherworldly charm.

Glass frogs aren't just fascinating to look at—they're also important to ecosystems. As insect-eaters, they help control pests, and their presence indicates healthy environments. But like many amphibians, they face threats from habitat loss and climate change, making them both biological oddities and conservation priorities.

Looking at a glass frog feels like peering into nature's laboratory, where every feature serves a purpose, even if it happens to be mesmerizingly strange. These delicate creatures remind us that evolution often produces beauty in the most unexpected ways.

The Dracula Ant's Jaw Speed

If ants held Olympic records, the Dracula ant would take gold every time. This tiny insect has jaws that snap shut at a mind-boggling 200 miles per hour, earning it the title of fastest recorded animal movement. To put that into perspective, it's 5,000 times faster than the blink of an eye and quicker than a high-speed train. Watching it in action would be thrilling—if only it weren't too fast for the naked eye.

But why does the Dracula ant need such turbocharged jaws? It's all about survival and sustenance. These ants use their lightning-fast mandibles to capture prey and protect their colonies. The mechanism works like a spring-loaded trap; the ants "cock" their jaws by pressing them together and then release the energy in a single explosive snap. It's precision engineering on a miniature scale, courtesy of evolution.

Despite its impressive speed, the Dracula ant isn't a bloodsucker. The name comes from its curious feeding habits: workers chew holes in their larvae and drink the hemolymph, or "ant blood," for nourishment. It sounds gruesome, but no harm comes to the larvae. In the world of ants, it's just another day at the office.

Tardigrades: The Indestructible Creatures

Tardigrades, affectionately known as water bears, are the superheroes of the microscopic world. These plump, eight-legged critters are practically indestructible, capable of surviving conditions that would obliterate most life forms. Extreme heat? No problem. Subzero temperatures? Bring it on. They've even endured the vacuum of space and lived to tell the tale—well, if they could talk.

Their secret lies in their ability to enter a state called cryptobiosis, where they lose almost all water from their bodies and essentially shut down their metabolism. In this state, tardigrades can endure radiation, dehydration, and even being frozen for decades. When conditions improve, they simply rehydrate and spring back to life as if nothing happened.

Though they're microscopic, tardigrades have captured the imaginations of scientists and the public alike. They've been sent to space, studied for their unique proteins, and even featured on T-shirts. These tiny titans remind us that resilience comes in all sizes, proving that even the smallest creatures can pack a serious punch.

The Mimic Octopus

In the world of camouflage, the mimic octopus is a master of disguise. Found in the murky waters of Southeast Asia, this clever cephalopod doesn't just blend in—it transforms, impersonating other marine animals to avoid predators. Whether it's a venomous lionfish, a sea snake, or a flatfish, the mimic octopus convincingly plays the part, complete with spot-on movements and behaviors.

This octopus's acting skills are so good that it often outwits even the most discerning predators. Threatened by a potential attacker? No problem—just morph into something scarier. Its ability to adapt its shape, color, and texture is unparalleled in the animal kingdom, making it both a marvel of evolution and an inspiration for countless nature documentaries.

The mimic octopus's talent isn't just for self-defense; it's also a tool for hunting. By impersonating prey species, it can sneak up on unsuspecting victims. It's as if the octopus carries a wardrobe of disguises, ready to adapt to any situation. With its combination of brains and beauty, the mimic octopus proves that sometimes, survival is all about being a drama queen.

The Shrimp That Shoots Boiling Water

The pistol shrimp might be small, but it packs a punch—literally. This tiny crustacean wields its claw like a firearm, creating a bubble that collapses with enough force to stun or kill prey. The snap of its claw generates temperatures briefly reaching 8,000°F, hotter than the surface of the sun. Talk about a hot shot!

The shrimp's "weapon" works by rapidly closing its specialized claw, which forces water out at high speed. This creates a cavitation bubble that bursts with a loud snap and a shockwave powerful enough to incapacitate nearby fish or crustaceans. The sound can reach up to 218 decibels, making it one of the loudest creatures in the ocean.

But the pistol shrimp isn't just a lone gunslinger. Many species live in symbiotic relationships with gobies, small fish that act as lookouts while the shrimp digs and maintains a shared burrow. It's a mutually beneficial partnership that pairs the shrimp's firepower with the goby's keen eyesight.

With its combination of explosive might and clever teamwork, the pistol shrimp is a testament to the ocean's knack for producing creatures that are as bizarre as they are brilliant. It's a reminder that in nature, even the smallest warriors can have the biggest impact.

The Planarian Flatworm's Memory Transfer

If flatworms had a motto, it might be: "What doesn't kill me makes me... two of me." Planarian flatworms are famous for their extraordinary regenerative abilities. Cut one in half, and both halves grow into fully functional worms. That's impressive enough, but here's the kicker: experiments suggest that both halves retain the memories of the original worm. Imagine waking up to find not only that you've been halved but that your other half knows your Netflix password.

Scientists tested this by training flatworms to navigate mazes and then cutting them into pieces. When the fragments regrew into full worms, they could still solve the maze as if they'd attended the same worm university. This phenomenon raises fascinating questions about where and how memories are stored. Is it in the brain, or does some aspect of memory reside in the body?

Planarian flatworms challenge our understanding of biology and cognition. They've become a staple of research into regeneration and memory, proving that even the simplest creatures can hold the most complex mysteries. If worms can multitask as regeneration experts and cognitive puzzles, who knows what secrets they're still keeping?

The Vampire Finch

The Galapagos Islands are home to some strange creatures, but few are as unexpected as the vampire finch. These small, unassuming birds have a surprisingly macabre diet: they drink blood. During the dry season, when food is scarce, the finches peck at the skin of larger seabirds, such as boobies, to feast on their blood. It's like nature's twisted version of a snack break.

While this behavior sounds horrifying, it's an ingenious survival strategy. The finches use their sharp beaks to pierce the seabirds' skin without causing significant harm, and the seabirds often tolerate it. Some scientists speculate that the finches initially learned this trick by eating parasites off the birds, only to develop a taste for the red stuff over time.

The vampire finch is a reminder of how resourceful nature can be, even when it veers into the creepy. It's also a testament to the unique evolutionary pressures of the Galapagos, where survival often hinges on adaptability. While the name might sound like a Halloween gimmick, the vampire finch is very real—and a little terrifying.

Self-Decapitating Sea Slugs

If you think quitting your job is dramatic, wait until you hear about the sea slug that quits its body. These extraordinary creatures, known as Elysia sea slugs, can voluntarily detach their heads from their bodies to escape parasites or other threats. But here's the real shocker: the head survives on its own and regenerates an entirely new body.

This bizarre process begins when the slug's head detaches and starts crawling around, leaving the old body to decompose. The head continues to feed on algae, extracting energy through photosynthesis, thanks to chloroplasts stolen from the algae. Over a few weeks, a shiny new body forms, complete with all the necessary organs.

Scientists are still puzzled by how these slugs manage such extreme regeneration. It's not just a biological curiosity—it could offer insights into medical advances, like regrowing organs or healing injuries. For now, the self-decapitating sea slug remains one of nature's most extreme survivalists, proving that sometimes, you just have to lose your head to stay ahead.

The Electric Eel's Shock Therapy

If the ocean had a power plant, it would be run by electric eels. These aquatic shockers can generate up to 600 volts of electricity, enough to light a small room—or deliver a jarring lesson to predators and prey. Despite their name, electric eels are actually a type of knifefish, not true eels, but their electric abilities are no less impressive.

Electric eels use specialized organs filled with electrocytes, cells that store and release electrical energy. By sending signals through these cells, the eel creates a powerful electric charge. It uses this ability for hunting, defense, and even navigation, emitting weak pulses to sense its surroundings in murky waters.

Perhaps the most astonishing feat is their hunting strategy. The eel emits a high-voltage shock to stun its prey, then follows up with a weaker pulse to confirm the prey's location. It's like nature's version of taser-meets-sonar, and it's ruthlessly effective.

While electric eels are fascinating, they're also a reminder to tread carefully in their territory. One shock won't kill you, but multiple jolts can be dangerous, especially if you're in water. These aquatic live wires are a perfect example of nature's ingenuity—an evolutionary marvel that reminds us never to underestimate the power of a good zap.

The Star-Nosed Mole's Super-Sniffer

The star-nosed mole looks like it belongs in a sci-fi movie, but this strange mammal is very much real—and its peculiar appearance serves a purpose. Found in wet lowlands of North America, the mole's distinctive star-shaped nose is a marvel of sensory engineering. Composed of 22 fleshy appendages covered in more than 25,000 tiny sensory receptors, this "nose" is the most sensitive tactile organ in the animal kingdom. It allows the mole to detect and consume prey in an astonishingly fast 120 milliseconds, making it the Usain Bolt of the mammal world when it comes to eating.

This bizarre-looking creature spends most of its time underground or underwater, where its super-nose helps it identify small invertebrates, worms, and aquatic prey. The mole's unique ability to "see" through touch is complemented by its surprising underwater sniffing technique, where it blows air bubbles and re-inhales them to detect scents. Yes, this mole can literally smell underwater.

Though it may not win any beauty contests, the star-nosed mole is a testament to evolution's creativity. It reminds us that nature often prioritizes function over form—and that weird is wonderful when it comes to survival.

The Hoatzin: The Stinky, Leaf-Eating Bird

Meet the hoatzin, a bird so odd that it's often referred to as the "stinkbird." Native to the Amazon Basin, this leaf-eating avian has a digestive system more akin to a cow's than a bird's. Instead of relying on a stomach filled with acid, the hoatzin ferments its food in a specialized crop, much like a bovine ruminant. While this adaptation allows it to subsist on a diet of leaves, it also gives the bird a pungent, manure-like odor.

But the hoatzin's weirdness doesn't stop at its smell. Baby hoatzins come equipped with tiny claws on their wings, a throwback to the age of dinosaurs. These claws help them climb trees when they're young, especially after jumping into water to evade predators—a bold escape tactic that earns them points for drama.

Despite its quirks, the hoatzin is an important part of its ecosystem, helping to maintain the balance of plant life along riverbanks. Love it or wrinkle your nose at it, the hoatzin is a feathered enigma that reminds us of evolution's unpredictable sense of humor.

Exploding Ants

Exploding ants might sound like a plot point from a bad sci-fi movie, but these tiny insects are the real deal. Found in

Southeast Asia, members of the Colobopsis genus have a defense mechanism that's as extreme as it is effective: they blow themselves up. When threatened, worker ants rupture their abdomens, releasing a sticky, toxic substance that immobilizes or repels attackers. It's a kamikaze tactic that protects the colony at the cost of the individual ant.

The ants' chemical arsenal isn't just randomly destructive—it's highly strategic. The goo they release contains substances that glue predators in place, giving their colony mates time to regroup and counterattack. Scientists are fascinated by this self-sacrificial behavior, which highlights the extreme lengths to which some species will go for collective survival.

While it might seem tragic, exploding ants thrive as a species, proving that sometimes, blowing up is the ultimate way to make an impact. They're a reminder that nature often prioritizes the group over the individual, even if it takes some explosive measures.

The Parasitic Tongue-Replacing Isopod

If you're squeamish, brace yourself for one of nature's most horrifying oddities: the tongue-replacing isopod. This parasitic crustacean attaches itself to a fish's tongue, drains its blood, and eventually takes the tongue's place. That's right—it becomes the fish's new tongue, functioning as a bizarre replacement organ for the rest of the fish's life.

The isopod's life cycle reads like a horror novel. It enters the fish through its gills, attaches to the base of the tongue, and feeds until the original tongue atrophies and falls off. Once installed, the isopod doesn't kill its host; it simply sits there, munching on scraps of food as the fish eats. In the parasite world, this is the ultimate example of "moving in and never leaving."

Despite its nightmarish lifestyle, the tongue-replacing isopod is harmless to humans and serves as a fascinating case study for scientists exploring symbiotic and parasitic relationships. For the fish, it's a peculiar inconvenience, but for us, it's a chilling reminder that the natural world often blurs the line between the bizarre and the grotesque.

Sociological Marvels

The Potlatch Ceremony

The potlatch ceremony, practiced by Indigenous peoples of the Pacific Northwest, flips traditional ideas of wealth on their head. In these elaborate gatherings, social status isn't gained by hoarding riches but by giving them away. A potlatch might include feasting, dancing, and storytelling, but the centerpiece is the host's extravagant distribution of goods. Blankets, food, and even canoes are handed out with the kind of generosity that would make a philanthropist blush.

This practice isn't just about showing off; it's deeply rooted in cultural values. By giving away wealth, hosts reinforce social bonds, assert leadership, and maintain communal harmony. It's an economic system based on reciprocity rather than accumulation, making it both an act of altruism and a strategic power play. Imagine hosting a dinner party and gaining lifelong respect by giving your guests your couch on the way out.

While European settlers misunderstood and even outlawed the potlatch for years, viewing it as wasteful, the ceremony survived as a resilient expression of cultural identity. Today, the potlatch continues to thrive as a testament to the enduring values of generosity and community. It's a powerful reminder that sometimes, giving it all away is the ultimate flex.

The Cargo Cults of Melanesia

Few sociological phenomena are as fascinating—and misunderstood—as the cargo cults of Melanesia. These emerged during and after World War II when Indigenous islanders observed Western soldiers unloading seemingly endless supplies of food, tools, and luxury goods from planes. To the Islanders, this "cargo" appeared to be a divine gift, and they sought to summon it by recreating the conditions they had witnessed.

Members of these cults built symbolic runways, control towers, and even mock planes out of bamboo and palm leaves, hoping to attract the mysterious "cargo gods." Rituals often included marching in formation or lighting signal fires, mimicking the behavior of the soldiers they'd seen. It was a sincere and creative attempt to understand and replicate an incomprehensible event within their worldview.

While often mocked as naïve by outsiders, cargo cults reveal a profound resilience and adaptability in human belief systems. They're a striking example of how people interpret the unknown through the lens of their culture, blending observation and spirituality. Far from being a quirky footnote in history, these movements challenge us to think about the cultural filters through which we all view the world.

The Matriarchal Society of the Mosuo

In a remote corner of China's Yunnan Province, the Mosuo people defy conventional norms with a matriarchal society that places women at the center of power. In the Mosuo's world, family lineage is traced through the mother, women control household finances, and "walking marriages" replace traditional unions. In these arrangements, men and women maintain separate homes, with men visiting their partners at night and returning to their mothers' households by morning.

This unconventional setup fosters remarkable social stability. Without cohabitation, there's no messy division of property or shared responsibilities to quarrel over. Children are raised by their mother's family, with uncles playing significant roles as male caregivers. The result is a tightly knit, matrilineal system that minimizes conflict and emphasizes communal bonds.

For the Mosuo, love and family are fluid, adaptable concepts. Their way of life offers a fascinating counterpoint to patriarchal norms, showing that societies can thrive under vastly different structures. While modern influences are slowly encroaching, the Mosuo's matriarchal traditions remain a compelling example of the diversity in human social systems—and a challenge to assumptions about what "normal" relationships look like.

Kibbutzim: The Collective Living Experiments

The kibbutzim of Israel are a sociological experiment in collective living that has endured for over a century. These cooperative communities were founded on socialist principles, with shared ownership of property, communal childcare, and collective labor. Members worked in agriculture, education, and manufacturing, pooling their resources for the common good. In the early days, they were a utopian ideal come to life, albeit with plenty of hard work and compromises.

Living on a kibbutz meant trading individual ambition for collective responsibility. Everyone contributed according to their abilities and received according to their needs. It sounds idyllic, but the reality wasn't without challenges. Personal privacy was limited, and tensions occasionally flared over resource distribution or individual freedoms.

Despite changes over time, including shifts toward privatization, many kibbutzim continue to thrive. They've adapted by incorporating more capitalist elements while maintaining their communal ethos. For sociologists, kibbutzim offer invaluable insights into how humans can balance cooperation and individuality in pursuit of a shared vision. These communities remain a fascinating case study in human ingenuity and the enduring appeal of collective living.

The Amish Rejection of Technology

In a world dominated by smartphones and streaming services, the Amish stand out as a community that says "no thanks" to modern technology. But their rejection of tech isn't about being anti-progress — it's about preserving a way of life that prioritizes family, faith, and community. The Amish use technology selectively, adopting tools that align with their values while avoiding those that might disrupt their close-knit lifestyle.

Take electricity, for example. Many Amish communities choose not to connect to the power grid, not because they hate lightbulbs, but because they believe it fosters dependency on the outside world. Instead, they rely on lanterns, horse-drawn carriages, and hand tools, creating a slower, more deliberate pace of life.

Despite appearances, the Amish aren't technophobic. They're pragmatists. Some use cell phones or power tools for business purposes but leave them outside the home to maintain domestic simplicity. This nuanced approach challenges the assumption that rejecting technology means rejecting modernity altogether. The Amish remind us that progress isn't always about having the latest gadget — it's about choosing the life you want to lead.

The Trobriand Islanders' Cricket Ritual

In the Trobriand Islands of Papua New Guinea, cricket is more than just a sport — it's a theatrical spectacle that fuses athleticism, ritual, and community spirit. Introduced by British missionaries in the early 20th century as a "civilizing" activity, cricket quickly evolved into something uniquely Trobriand. Forget stiff-upper-lip sportsmanship; here, matches include dances, chants, and elaborate displays of cultural pride.

The Trobriand version of cricket is rich with symbolism. Teams perform warlike chants and dances before matches, brandishing bats like clubs in a display of controlled aggression. Instead of the stoic clapping of traditional cricket, points are celebrated with jubilant performances, and outcomes are less about competition and more about showcasing skill and unity.

Even the rules have been adapted. Matches often include more than the usual two teams, and scoring can be... flexible. The game's primary goal isn't winning but honoring traditions, strengthening social ties, and expressing creativity. In a way, Trobriand cricket turns a colonial pastime into a celebration of cultural resilience, reminding us that sports can be much more than just a game.

The Ik People of Uganda

The Ik people of Uganda offer one of the most sobering examples of human adaptability in extreme conditions. Living in the rugged mountains near the Kenyan border, the Ik have faced generations of hardship due to environmental degradation, famine, and displacement. Anthropologist Colin Turnbull's 1972 book The Mountain People portrayed them as shockingly individualistic, a society where every man, woman, and child fends for themselves.

Turnbull's grim account described a community where even family bonds had frayed under the pressure of scarcity. Parents would abandon children too weak to contribute, and individuals hoarded food rather than share. However, modern researchers have revisited the Ik, finding a more nuanced picture. While individualism remains a strong trait, the Ik also exhibit moments of cooperation and resilience, suggesting that Turnbull's observations were shaped by the extreme conditions at the time.

The Ik remind us that human behavior is deeply shaped by environment and circumstance. Their story challenges simplistic views of morality, showing how survival can reshape even the most fundamental social bonds.

The Haka Dance in New Zealand

The haka is more than a dance—it's a roar of identity, pride, and unity. Traditionally performed by the Māori of New Zealand, the haka is a war dance originally used to intimidate enemies on the battlefield. Its fierce movements, rhythmic chanting, and intense facial expressions—sticking out tongues and bulging eyes included—make it impossible to ignore.

Today, the haka is far more than a relic of warfare. It's performed at weddings, funerals, and, most famously, sporting events. New Zealand's All Blacks rugby team has brought the haka to the global stage, using it as a pre-match ritual to psych themselves up and, let's face it, terrify their opponents.

The haka transcends its original purpose, becoming a universal symbol of strength and cultural pride. It's a way for Māori communities to preserve their heritage and assert their identity in a modern world. Watching a haka is a visceral experience, a reminder that movement and sound can communicate power in ways words never could.

The Bhutanese Gross National Happiness Index

Forget GDP—Bhutan measures its success through Gross National Happiness (GNH). This Himalayan kingdom decided long ago that prosperity isn't just about money; it's about well-being, sustainability, and cultural preservation. Introduced in the 1970s by Bhutan's fourth king, GNH evaluates progress through four pillars: sustainable development, environmental conservation, cultural preservation, and good governance.

This holistic approach has led Bhutan to prioritize green energy, ban plastic bags, and limit mass tourism to protect its pristine environment. But GNH isn't just about policies; it's a philosophy deeply rooted in Buddhist values. Happiness is considered a communal goal, not an individual pursuit, making Bhutan an inspiring case study for nations grappling with the downsides of unchecked economic growth.

While skeptics question how happiness can truly be measured, Bhutan's commitment to its people's well-being offers a refreshing counterpoint to conventional metrics. In a world that often equates success with profit, Bhutan reminds us that contentment and connection might just be the ultimate wealth.

The Nomadic Sea Gypsies of Southeast Asia

The nomadic Sea Gypsies, or Bajau, are a community of maritime wanderers who have lived for generations almost entirely at sea. Found in the waters of Southeast Asia, particularly around Indonesia, Malaysia, and the Philippines, the Bajau are famed for their free-diving abilities. With no modern diving equipment, they can hold their breath for minutes at a time and dive to depths of over 200 feet, a skill honed through centuries of living in harmony with the ocean.

Scientists have discovered that the Bajau possess physiological adaptations that make them exceptional divers, including enlarged spleens that store extra oxygenated red blood cells. These unique traits are a testament to how human bodies can adapt to extreme environments over time.

Despite their incredible abilities, the Bajau face challenges as modernity encroaches on their traditional way of life. Pollution, overfishing, and political pressures threaten their nomadic existence. Yet, they remain a symbol of humanity's deep connection to the sea—a reminder that we're capable of extraordinary feats when we live in sync with our environment.

The Barefoot College in India

In a small village in Rajasthan, India, there's a college where students carry no books, wear no uniforms, and learn by doing rather than reading. The Barefoot College, founded in 1972, is a revolutionary institution designed to empower illiterate women from rural areas by teaching them practical skills like solar engineering. Here, grandmothers from around the world—many of whom have never been to school—learn to install and maintain solar panels, lighting up not just their villages but their futures.

The approach is as innovative as it is inclusive. Classes are conducted through hands-on demonstrations and universal symbols, bypassing the barriers of language and literacy. By the time they graduate, these women, often called "solar mamas," return home equipped to bring electricity to their communities. The ripple effects are transformative, reducing dependence on kerosene lamps, improving health, and creating a sense of self-reliance in regions often overlooked by traditional education.

The Barefoot College isn't just a school; it's a movement. It proves that education doesn't have to fit conventional molds to create lasting change. By tapping into the potential of those society often ignores, it's lighting a path—literally and metaphorically—for a brighter future.

The Zulu Bead Language

In Zulu culture, jewelry isn't just decorative—it's a form of communication. Known as Zulu bead language, this intricate system uses patterns, colors, and arrangements of beads to convey emotions, social status, and even romantic intentions. Think of it as texting, but far more artistic and subtle.

Each color carries specific meanings: white symbolizes purity, blue represents faithfulness, and red signifies love or strong emotions. When combined into patterns, these beads can tell detailed stories. For example, a triangle pointing upward in a necklace indicates an unmarried man, while one pointing downward signifies a single woman. A clever mix of designs can deliver anything from a marriage proposal to a gentle rejection, all without uttering a word.

Zulu bead language isn't just a romantic tool; it's a cultural treasure that preserves traditions and fosters connection within the community. In an era of instant messaging, it's refreshing to think of a world where every bead counts, and conversations are as timeless as the art itself.

The Mehinaku and Their Love Huts

Deep in the Amazon rainforest, the Mehinaku tribe has a unique take on romance. Among their many customs, one of the most fascinating is the "love hut." These temporary structures are built specifically for romantic encounters, providing a private space for couples to connect away from the watchful eyes of the village.

The concept might sound unusual to outsiders, but in the close-knit world of the Mehinaku, where daily life revolves around communal living, privacy is a rare luxury. Love huts offer an escape for couples to explore their relationships without the interference of family dynamics or village gossip.

While the idea of constructing a hut for love may seem labor-intensive, it reflects the importance of intimacy and respect within Mehinaku society. It's a practical solution to a universal need: the chance to be alone together. The love hut is a reminder that no matter where we live, some things — like the desire for connection — transcend culture and geography.

The Mysterious Green Children of Woolpit

One of the strangest tales from medieval England is the legend of the green children of Woolpit. According to 12th-century accounts, two children with green-tinted skin appeared in the Suffolk village, speaking an unknown language and wearing unfamiliar clothes. The boy and girl claimed to come from a subterranean land called "St. Martin's Land," where the sun never shone, and everything was bathed in twilight.

The story takes an even stranger turn. The children were taken in by a local family, and over time, their green hue faded as they adapted to a diet of bread and other local fare. Sadly, the boy didn't survive long, but the girl grew up, learned English, and explained that they had wandered into Woolpit through a cave after becoming lost.

Historians and folklorists have debated the tale's origins for centuries, with theories ranging from malnutrition causing the green tint to more fantastical ideas of interdimensional travel. Whether fact, fiction, or a mix of both, the green children of Woolpit remain an enduring mystery that continues to capture imaginations.

The Balinese Nyepi Day (Day of Silence)

Once a year, the entire island of Bali falls silent. Known as Nyepi Day, this Hindu New Year celebration is unlike any other. From sunrise to sunrise, no one works, travels, or even turns on the lights. The streets are empty, the beaches are deserted, and an eerie hush falls over the usually bustling island.

The purpose of Nyepi is to cleanse the island of evil spirits. Balinese believe that by creating a scene of complete inactivity, they can trick malevolent entities into thinking the island is uninhabited, convincing them to leave. It's like playing a cosmic game of hide-and-seek, and the stakes couldn't be higher.

For locals and visitors alike, Nyepi is an opportunity for reflection and spiritual renewal. Families stay home, meditate, and enjoy a rare day of uninterrupted quiet. The night sky, free from light pollution, becomes a dazzling display of stars, reminding everyone of their place in the universe.

Nyepi is more than just a cultural practice—it's a profound act of collective mindfulness. In a world that never seems to stop, Bali's Day of Silence is a refreshing reminder that sometimes, the best way to move forward is to pause.

The "Day of the Dead" in Mexico

The "Day of the Dead," or Día de los Muertos, is not your typical somber affair. Instead, it's a vibrant celebration of life, death, and the enduring bond between the two. Taking place on November 1st and 2nd, this Mexican tradition blends indigenous practices with Catholic influences, creating a cultural event that's both deeply spiritual and joyously festive.

During the holiday, families build ofrendas (altars) adorned with photos, marigolds, candles, and offerings like food and drinks to welcome back the spirits of their loved ones. The favorite dishes of the deceased, from tamales to tequila, are lovingly prepared, because even in the afterlife, everyone appreciates good food. It's a time to laugh, share stories, and remember the lives of those who've passed.

Perhaps the most iconic symbol of the celebration is the sugar skull, or calavera. These colorful confections, often personalized, symbolize the sweetness and inevitability of life's cycle. The festival, famously depicted in films like Coco, invites both locals and tourists to embrace death not as an end but as a continuation of life's journey. In its exuberant mix of reverence and revelry, the Day of the Dead offers a profound lesson: cherish your loved ones while they're here, and celebrate them when they're gone.

The Cooperative Markets of Mondragón, Spain

Nestled in Spain's Basque Country, the town of Mondragón has redefined capitalism with a unique network of worker-owned cooperatives. Established in 1956, this system operates on the principles of shared ownership, democratic decision-making, and community-focused growth. Employees aren't just workers—they're co-owners, sharing profits and responsibilities equally. In a world often driven by cutthroat competition, Mondragón stands as a beacon of economic collaboration.

The cooperative model thrives on inclusivity. From industrial manufacturing to education and finance, Mondragón's cooperatives cover a wide range of industries, all working together in mutual support. Workers vote on major decisions, including salaries, which helps to maintain equality and minimize the stark pay gaps seen in traditional corporate structures.

Mondragón's success isn't just theoretical—it's practical. Even during economic downturns, these cooperatives have demonstrated remarkable resilience by prioritizing job retention and resource-sharing over layoffs. It's a living example that business doesn't have to be a zero-sum game, proving that collective prosperity is possible.

The San People and the Click Languages

The San people of southern Africa are often called the "first people" due to their deep connection to humanity's origins. Among their many cultural wonders is their language, which features distinctive click sounds that are as fascinating as they are challenging for outsiders to mimic. These clicks, produced by sharp movements of the tongue against the teeth or roof of the mouth, add a musical quality to the San's speech.

Click languages are not only unique but ancient, offering a window into the earliest forms of human communication. Linguists believe the complexity of these languages points to their deep evolutionary roots, making them a living museum of linguistic history. Despite their beauty, these languages face the threat of extinction as modern influences encroach on San culture.

The San people's connection to their environment is as rich as their language. Known for their extraordinary tracking skills and intimate knowledge of the land, they embody a way of life that has endured for tens of thousands of years. Their language and traditions remind us of humanity's shared past and the intricate tapestry of cultures that shaped it.

The Quinceañera in Latin America

A quinceañera is more than a birthday party—it's a rite of passage, a cultural cornerstone, and an excuse for a really fabulous dress. Celebrated in many Latin American cultures, this event marks a girl's 15th birthday, symbolizing her transition from childhood to womanhood. Part debutante ball, part family reunion, and part spiritual milestone, the quinceañera is steeped in tradition.

The celebration typically begins with a Catholic mass, where the young woman thanks God for her life and receives blessings for her future. Dressed in an elaborate gown that would make Cinderella jealous, she then takes center stage at a lavish reception featuring dancing, speeches, and, often, a choreographed waltz with her father.

But the quinceañera isn't just about glitz and glamour—it's a deeply symbolic event. From the presentation of a doll, signifying the end of childhood, to the ceremonial exchange of flat shoes for high heels, every element carries meaning. It's a celebration of family, faith, and community, all wrapped in a glittering bow.

The Long Neck Women of the Padaung Tribe

The Padaung women of Myanmar are instantly recognizable by the brass coils they wear around their necks, creating the illusion of elongation. While often called "giraffe women," this tradition is deeply rooted in cultural identity rather than zoological imitation. The coils, first added during childhood, are gradually increased over the years, compressing the collarbone and giving the neck a stretched appearance.

For the Padaung, the coils are a symbol of beauty and status. They're also believed to have spiritual significance, offering protection from harm. Despite misconceptions, the practice doesn't actually "stretch" the neck—it alters the rib cage, creating the elongated effect.

Still, for many Padaung women, the coils are a source of pride, embodying the enduring beauty of their cultural heritage.

Psychological Phenomena

The Mandela Effect

Have you ever sworn something was true only to discover you and countless others were completely wrong? Welcome to the Mandela Effect, a psychological phenomenon that proves memory is not the steel trap we'd like to believe it is. Named after Nelson Mandela, this effect originated from widespread false memories of his death in prison in the 1980s—despite the fact that he was very much alive until 2013.

Examples abound, from the "Berenstain Bears" vs. "Berenstein Bears" debate to the collective misremembering of the Monopoly Man having a monocle (he doesn't). Some blame it on parallel universes colliding or glitches in the matrix, while psychologists point to cognitive biases, social reinforcement, and the malleable nature of memory itself.

The Mandela Effect is both a fascinating and humbling reminder of how easily our minds can play tricks on us. It's a shared experience that makes us question not only the past but our perception of reality. And honestly, wouldn't life be a little dull without these little brain hiccups?

The Placebo Effect

Imagine taking a sugar pill and feeling your headache vanish. That's the placebo effect—a testament to the astonishing power of belief. This psychological phenomenon occurs when an inactive treatment produces real physical or emotional improvements simply because the person expects it to work.

Placebos aren't just confined to pills; they extend to fake surgeries, sham acupuncture, and even inert creams. The secret sauce lies in the brain's ability to release chemicals like endorphins in response to positive expectations. Essentially, your mind becomes the ultimate pharmacist.

While the placebo effect is often associated with trickery, it has real therapeutic potential. Researchers are exploring how it can be harnessed to reduce reliance on medications or enhance treatment outcomes. It's a quirky reminder that sometimes, believing in the cure is half the battle.

Synesthesia: Mixed Senses

What if Thursdays were green, Beethoven tasted like chocolate, or the number 7 felt prickly? Welcome to the world of synesthesia, where senses intermingle in a dazzling display of crosswired perception. For people with synesthesia, everyday experiences are enhanced—or perhaps complicated—by automatic and involuntary sensory overlap.

This neurological condition comes in many flavors. Grapheme-color synesthetes see numbers or letters as specific colors, while chromesthesia causes sounds to evoke vivid visual experiences. It's not just a quirk; synesthesia is often linked to creativity. Some famous synesthetes include composer Franz Liszt and artist Wassily Kandinsky, who credited their unique perceptions with shaping their art.

Far from being a disorder, synesthesia is often celebrated as a fascinating variation in how humans experience the world. It challenges our understanding of the brain's sensory boundaries, proving that reality is, quite literally, in the eye—and ear, and tongue—of the beholder.

Déjà Vu

Déjà vu is like a glitch in the brain's matrix. It's that fleeting, spine-tingling sensation of having already experienced a moment you know is happening for the first time. For a few disorienting seconds, reality feels like a rerun, leaving you questioning the very fabric of time and space.

Scientists have several theories about déjà vu, but no definitive answers. Some suggest it's a misfire in the brain's memory system, where new experiences are mistakenly processed as familiar. Others speculate it's a trick of attention, where a brief lapse in focus makes the present feel like the past. Whatever the cause, it's a universal quirk that has perplexed humans for centuries.

While déjà vu might feel like a brush with the supernatural, it's more likely a reminder of how complex—and occasionally buggy—our brains can be. And honestly, isn't life a little more exciting with the occasional déjà vu mystery thrown in?

The Spotlight Effect

Ever felt like everyone was staring at you because of a bad hair day or a coffee stain on your shirt? That's the spotlight effect at work, the psychological bias that makes us believe we're the star of everyone else's attention. The reality? Most people are too busy worrying about their own metaphorical coffee stains to notice yours.

The spotlight effect stems from our egocentric perspective, where we overestimate how much others focus on us. Studies show that we're far less scrutinized than we imagine, yet the belief persists, fueling social anxiety and self-consciousness.

Understanding the spotlight effect can be liberating. Realizing that people aren't dissecting your every move frees you to embrace imperfections and live with less worry. After all, if everyone's busy thinking about themselves, you might as well do the same — just with less stress and more confidence.

Learned Helplessness

Imagine a dog in a cage with a floor that delivers random electric shocks. The dog eventually stops trying to escape, even when the door is left open. This unsettling experiment by psychologist Martin Seligman in the 1960s gave us the term "learned helplessness." The concept describes a mental state where repeated failure or adversity convinces individuals that they are powerless to change their circumstances — even when opportunities for change are available.

Humans, unfortunately, are just as susceptible. Whether it's a student giving up on math after failing a few tests or someone staying in an unhealthy relationship, learned helplessness can creep in when setbacks pile up. The belief that nothing can be done becomes a self-fulfilling prophecy, creating a vicious cycle of inaction.

The good news is that learned helplessness isn't permanent. Therapy, encouragement, and positive reinforcement can help people break free from this mental trap. The lesson? Failure isn't final — it's just a pit stop on the road to resilience.

Cognitive Dissonance

Cognitive dissonance is what happens when your brain has an internal argument with itself. It's the discomfort you feel when your actions contradict your beliefs or when two conflicting ideas fight for dominance. For example, if you believe in healthy eating but find yourself devouring a box of donuts, you might justify it by saying, "It's fine; I'll work out tomorrow."

This psychological phenomenon, first explored by Leon Festinger in the 1950s, is a masterclass in mental gymnastics. To reduce the discomfort, we either change our behavior, adjust our beliefs, or come up with creative excuses. Cognitive dissonance is why smokers rationalize their habit ("It keeps me calm!") and why people defend questionable purchases ("I needed that overpriced gadget").

While cognitive dissonance can be unsettling, it's also a powerful motivator for change. Recognizing it can help us align our actions with our values—or at least come up with better excuses for our donut binges.

The Baader-Meinhof Phenomenon

Ever learn a new word and suddenly see it everywhere? That's the Baader-Meinhof Phenomenon, also called the "frequency illusion." It's like the universe is playing tricks on you, but in reality, it's your brain's heightened awareness of something it just learned.

The phenomenon occurs because of selective attention and confirmation bias. Once your brain deems something significant, it unconsciously starts noticing it more. For instance, you learn about a rare breed of dog, and suddenly, every park seems filled with them. The dogs were always there; your brain just decided to pay attention.

While the Baader-Meinhof Phenomenon can make you feel like a character in a cosmic joke, it's a fascinating reminder of how our minds filter and prioritize information. It's not magic—it's just your brain's way of keeping the world interesting.

The Bystander Effect

Picture this: a crowd gathers as someone yells for help, but no one steps in. That's the bystander effect, a psychological phenomenon where the presence of others reduces the likelihood that any one person will intervene in an emergency. It's the ultimate case of "someone else will do it."

First studied after the infamous 1964 murder of Kitty Genovese, the bystander effect reveals a paradox: the more people around, the less likely anyone is to act. This happens due to diffusion of responsibility—each person assumes someone else will step up. Ironically, in smaller groups, people are more likely to help because there's no one else to pass the buck.

Understanding the bystander effect is empowering. Knowing it exists can help us overcome it, reminding us that sometimes, it's up to you to break the cycle of inaction.

Phantom Limb Syndrome

Losing a limb doesn't mean losing sensation—at least not for the brain. Phantom limb syndrome is a phenomenon where amputees continue to feel pain, itching, or other sensations in the missing limb. It's as if the brain refuses to acknowledge the limb's absence, clinging stubbornly to its original neural map.

The sensations can be eerily realistic, ranging from the feeling of a hand clenching to the burn of an itch that can't be scratched. This happens because the brain's sensory and motor regions, once responsible for the limb, are still active. Sometimes, nearby neural networks "invade" the unused area, leading to mixed signals and strange sensations.

While phantom limb syndrome can be distressing, treatments like mirror therapy offer relief. By tricking the brain into "seeing" the missing limb through a mirror reflection, patients can often reduce pain and regain a sense of control. It's a testament to the brain's adaptability and its occasional stubborn refusal to let go.

Pareidolia: Seeing Faces in Objects

Ever see a smile in your morning toast or a pair of eyes staring back from your car's headlights? That's pareidolia in action, a delightful quirk of the human brain that compels us to find familiar patterns—especially faces—in random stimuli. It's why clouds can look like dragons, the Moon is said to have a "man," and some people swear they see Elvis in a potato chip.

Pareidolia isn't just about faces; it's about our brain's constant search for order in chaos. This instinct likely evolved for survival. Recognizing a face in the bushes could mean spotting a friend—or a foe—before it's too late. Today, it's less about survival and more about entertainment. Who hasn't laughed at a houseplant that looks suspiciously grumpy?

Artists and marketers also love pareidolia. Logos and product designs often exploit our tendency to anthropomorphize objects, creating emotional connections. It's proof that our brains are endlessly creative, even if they sometimes get carried away.

The Hawthorne Effect

The Hawthorne Effect is the psychological equivalent of "smile, you're on camera!" It describes how people change their behavior simply because they know they're being observed. The phenomenon gets its name from a 1920s study at Western Electric's Hawthorne Works, where workers increased productivity regardless of changes in lighting or working conditions — because they felt watched.

While the original study has been critiqued, the effect remains a powerful reminder of how much we crave approval. Knowing someone's paying attention can make us try harder, whether it's a boss monitoring performance or a friend cheering us on.

On the flip side, the Hawthorne Effect can skew research results. In experiments, participants might behave unnaturally just to impress the researcher. It's a lesson in the power of perception — sometimes, just being noticed is enough to bring out our best (or most self-conscious) selves.

The Tetris Effect

Play Tetris for hours, and suddenly, everything looks like falling blocks. This phenomenon, aptly named the Tetris Effect, occurs when a repetitive activity starts to dominate your thoughts, dreams, and even how you perceive the world. It's not limited to Tetris; spend enough time knitting, and you might "see" stitches in everyday patterns.

The Tetris Effect reveals how deeply our brains absorb repetitive tasks. It's not just a quirk — it's a reflection of neural plasticity, the brain's ability to adapt and reorganize itself. While it might seem odd to dream about aligning bricks, this phenomenon can have practical benefits. For instance, studies show that playing Tetris after a traumatic event can reduce flashbacks, suggesting it can redirect mental energy in positive ways.

So the next time you find yourself mentally organizing grocery shelves into perfect rows, embrace it. Your brain is just doing what it does best: turning life into a puzzle.

Procrastination and the "Present Bias"

Ah, procrastination—the art of delaying today what can easily stress you out tomorrow. At its core lies the "present bias," our tendency to prioritize immediate rewards over long-term benefits. Why start that report now when you can binge-watch a series and worry about deadlines later?

The problem with present bias is that it creates a tug-of-war between short-term satisfaction and long-term goals. Our brains are wired to favor instant gratification because it feels good now. Unfortunately, future-you is often left cleaning up the mess, wondering why past-you thought scrolling through memes was a good idea.

The solution? Strategies like breaking tasks into smaller steps or rewarding yourself for progress. Procrastination isn't just laziness—it's a universal struggle between impulse and intention. Understanding it can turn the battle into a manageable truce.

The IKEA Effect

If you've ever assembled an IKEA bookshelf and felt a strange sense of pride (despite leftover screws), you've experienced the IKEA Effect. This psychological quirk describes how we place higher value on things we've partially created ourselves. It's why homemade cookies taste better than store-bought ones—or why that slightly wobbly table feels like an heirloom.

The IKEA Effect happens because effort increases attachment. When we invest time and energy into something, we become emotionally connected to it, even if the end result isn't perfect. Companies like IKEA have capitalized on this by turning customers into co-creators. By the time you've spent hours deciphering instructions and wielding an Allen wrench, that bookshelf isn't just furniture—it's yours.

This phenomenon isn't just about flatpacks; it's a reminder that effort and value are intertwined. Whether it's a project, a relationship, or a wobbly table, what we put into something shapes how much it's worth to us. And maybe those leftover screws are just a bonus.

Imposter Syndrome

Imposter syndrome is the mental equivalent of waiting for someone to tap you on the shoulder and say, "We've discovered your secret—you don't belong here." It's a persistent, nagging belief that your success is a fluke, despite all evidence to the contrary. From high-achieving students to accomplished professionals, it spares no one. Even famous figures like Maya Angelou and Albert Einstein admitted to feeling like frauds at times.

The irony is that imposter syndrome thrives in capable people, feeding off their self-doubt. Did you ace that presentation? Must've been luck. Got promoted? Clearly a mistake. This inner critic is relentless, dismissing hard work and talent while magnifying every minor misstep.

The truth? Imposter syndrome lies. Success isn't about knowing everything—it's about showing up, learning, and growing. Recognizing this can help quiet that voice of doubt. And remember, if Einstein felt like a fraud, maybe it's just a sign you're in great company.

The Pygmalion Effect

The Pygmalion Effect proves that expectations are powerful. Named after the Greek myth of Pygmalion, who sculpted a statue so perfect it came to life, this psychological phenomenon occurs when high expectations lead to improved performance. If someone believes you're capable, chances are you'll rise to meet that belief.

In classrooms, teachers who expect students to excel often see better results, not because the students suddenly grow smarter but because the encouragement boosts their confidence and motivation. It's a feedback loop of positivity: belief fosters effort, which fosters success.

The Pygmalion Effect is a reminder that words and attitudes matter. Whether you're a teacher, boss, or friend, your expectations can shape outcomes in surprising ways. So, expect greatness — it might just come true.

The Rubber Hand Illusion

The Rubber Hand Illusion is a party trick for your brain — and it's weirdly convincing. In this sensory experiment, a fake rubber hand is placed in front of you while your real hand is hidden. Both are stroked simultaneously with a brush, and within minutes, your brain adopts the rubber hand as its own.

This illusion highlights how easily our sense of body ownership can be fooled. The brain prioritizes synchronized sensory input over reality, effectively saying, "If it feels like mine, it must be mine." Researchers have even taken this further, using virtual reality or prosthetics to explore how our brains map the body.

While it's fun to watch someone flinch when the rubber hand is "injured," the Rubber Hand Illusion also has practical applications in rehabilitation and prosthetics. It's a quirky reminder that our brains are both brilliant and hilariously gullible.

The McGurk Effect

What happens when your eyes and ears disagree? Welcome to the McGurk Effect, a phenomenon where visual cues, like lip movements, influence what we hear. For example, watching someone say "ba" while their lips form "fa" often makes you hear "fa" instead. It's sensory confusion at its finest.

This effect demonstrates how much we rely on vision to interpret sound. In noisy environments, we unconsciously lip-read to enhance comprehension. But when visual and auditory inputs clash, the brain blends them, creating an entirely new perception.

The McGurk Effect is a fascinating quirk of human perception, proving that what we see can change what we hear. It's also a great reminder to double-check your senses—sometimes, they conspire against you.

Hyperthymesia: Superior Autobiographical Memory

Imagine remembering every detail of every day of your life: the weather on a random Tuesday ten years ago, what you ate, and the exact outfit you wore. That's the reality for people with hyperthymesia, a rare condition that grants near-perfect autobiographical memory.

Hyperthymesiacs, like actress Marilu Henner, describe their memories as a constant mental playback.

It's not a photographic memory, which recalls everything; hyperthymesia is highly specific to personal experiences. While fascinating, it's not without challenges. Reliving every joy also means revisiting every heartbreak, often in vivid detail.

For researchers, hyperthymesia offers a unique glimpse into how memory works. These individuals show us what's possible when the brain doesn't let go, even if it sometimes feels like a blessing and a curse.

It's a superpower of recall, but like any power, it comes with its own complexities.

Economic Peculiarities

Tulip Mania: The First Economic Bubble

In 17th-century Netherlands, tulips weren't just flowers—they were status symbols, and the Dutch fell for them like lovesick teenagers. Tulip mania, often cited as the first recorded economic bubble, saw prices for these coveted bulbs skyrocket to absurd levels. By the peak in the mid-1630s, a single tulip bulb could cost more than a skilled artisan's annual salary—or, in some cases, the price of a house.

But what goes up must come down, and tulips proved no exception. By 1637, the market collapsed. Buyers suddenly realized they'd traded fortunes for... well, flowers. The fallout left many in financial ruin, and the event became a cautionary tale about speculative investing.

Today, tulip mania is a reminder that even the most sensible-seeming people can lose their minds over fleeting trends. It's a story that still resonates in modern markets—just replace tulips with tech stocks, cryptocurrencies, or beanie babies.

The Yap Stone Money

Imagine paying for groceries with a coin so large it requires a forklift. On the Micronesian island of Yap, that's not far from reality. The Yapese use massive limestone disks, known as rai, as currency. Some are as big as 12 feet in diameter and weigh several tons.

Interestingly, these stones often never move. Ownership is transferred verbally, with the stones remaining in place, a testament to the Yapese trust system. One famously "lost" rai is at the bottom of the ocean after a canoe accident—but it's still considered valid currency because everyone agrees it's there.

Rai stones symbolize value beyond practicality, showcasing how culture, not utility, defines money. It's a quirky, enduring system that turns the concept of portable currency on its head— or its very large side.

The Zimbabwe Billion-Dollar Note

Few symbols of hyperinflation are as jaw-dropping as Zimbabwe's $100 trillion note. In the late 2000s, Zimbabwe faced catastrophic inflation rates, peaking at a mind-boggling 89.7 sextillion percent. Basic goods like bread required wheelbarrows of cash, while the value of the currency plummeted to near nothing.

The $100 trillion note became a bizarre relic of the crisis. Once worth less than a loaf of bread, it's now a sought-after collector's item. Ironically, it's probably worth more as a novelty than it ever was as currency.

Zimbabwe's story serves as a stark lesson in economic mismanagement and the fragility of trust in money. For the rest of us, it's also a reminder that carrying smaller denominations isn't always a bad thing.

Beaver Pelts as Currency in Colonial Canada

In early Canadian settlements, forget gold or paper money— beaver pelts were the real currency. In the 17th and 18th centuries, the fur trade dominated the economy, with beaver pelts prized for their use in felt hats. A beaver pelt wasn't just a luxury item; it was a unit of trade.

Trappers exchanged pelts for goods like tools, fabric, and even liquor, creating an economy where the value of a hat rested on the back of a rodent. Indigenous peoples were integral to this system, trading pelts for European goods and building cross-cultural alliances — albeit ones often marred by exploitation.

Beaver pelts became so valuable that the Hudson's Bay Company used them as a standard of trade, cementing the furry currency's place in history. Today, it's a quaint reminder of a time when a good hat was worth its weight in beaver.

The Price of Witches in Salem

The Salem Witch Trials of 1692 weren't just about superstition — they were also steeped in economics. The infamous hysteria, which saw 20 people executed and over 200 accused, was fueled in part by land disputes and economic tension.

Salem's community was divided between prosperous merchants in the bustling town and struggling farmers in the rural outskirts. Accusations often aligned with these divides, as land disputes turned into witch hunts. By accusing a neighbor of witchcraft, individuals could gain control of valuable property, making witch trials a gruesome form of economic warfare.

While religious fervor and paranoia were central to the trials, the economic backdrop provides a chilling lens on how financial pressures can amplify societal fractures. It's a haunting reminder that even witch hunts can have dollar signs lurking in the shadows.

The Salt Economy of Ancient Rome

Imagine a world where salt wasn't just a seasoning but a form of currency. For Roman soldiers, this was reality. The word "salary" actually comes from the Latin salarium, a term linked to the practice of paying soldiers with salt or an allowance to buy it. Salt was so valuable that it was often referred to as "white gold," critical for preserving food in an era before refrigeration.

Roman armies needed salt not just for their own diets but also to sustain their horses and livestock. Controlling salt supplies was a matter of military strategy, with access often determining the success of campaigns. Some historians argue that salt's importance shaped trade routes and even the outcomes of wars.

While we may take salt for granted today, its role in ancient economies underscores how something as seemingly mundane as seasoning could once carry such weight—literally. So next time you sprinkle salt on your fries, remember, you're enjoying a luxury once worth marching an army for.

Bitcoin Pizza Day

In May 2010, a Florida man named Laszlo Hanyecz made history by trading 10,000 Bitcoins for two pizzas. At the time, Bitcoin was a novelty, valued at fractions of a cent. Hanyecz's transaction marked the first real-world purchase using cryptocurrency, but it's since become a cautionary tale of missed opportunity. Those 10,000 Bitcoins would now be worth hundreds of millions of dollars.

Bitcoin Pizza Day is celebrated annually in the crypto community as a reminder of how far the currency has come— and how deliciously undervalued it once was. It's also a lesson in hindsight: while Hanyecz's pizzas were probably tasty, they've become the world's most expensive slices.

The story highlights Bitcoin's journey from geeky experiment to global financial player, proving that sometimes, even pizza can be revolutionary.

Cowry Shells as Global Currency

Cowry shells, small and shiny, might seem like trinkets today, but for centuries, they served as currency across Africa, Asia, and the Pacific. Lightweight, durable, and easy to count, cowries were ideal for trade. They were even referred to as the "currency of the Indian Ocean," facilitating exchanges from gold to spices.

Their value wasn't just practical; it was cultural. In some societies, cowries symbolized wealth and power, often adorning royal garments and ceremonial items. They were a versatile currency long before coins or paper money became widespread.

The cowry economy demonstrates that money's value is as much about perception as utility. These humble shells connected vast trade networks, proving that even small things can hold big significance in global history.

The Great Depression and the Glass Eel Boom

During the Great Depression, economic hardship forced people to get creative. Enter the glass eel, a slippery, translucent fish that became an unexpected commodity. These eels, prized for their flavor and ability to thrive in aquaculture, were caught and sold to boost incomes when traditional jobs disappeared.

In places like Europe and Japan, glass eels became a delicacy, fueling demand that turned them into a thriving export industry. Communities near rivers saw their fortunes tied to the seasonal migration of these tiny creatures, whose value grew as natural stocks dwindled.

The glass eel boom is a reminder that even in the hardest times, resourcefulness can turn the smallest things — quite literally — into economic lifelines. It's also proof that the Great Depression wasn't all dust bowls and despair; there was some fishy business, too.

Frequent Flyer Miles as Currency

Frequent flyer miles started as a marketing gimmick but have since evolved into a valuable, tradeable asset. Originally intended to reward airline loyalty, miles have become their own economy, allowing savvy travelers to score flights, upgrades, and even merchandise.

What's fascinating is how these miles now function as a quasi-currency. Some people buy, sell, or even hoard them like treasure, with entire websites and consultants dedicated to maximizing their value. The miles' worth fluctuates depending on airline policies, making them subject to inflation much like traditional currency.

Frequent flyer miles showcase the power of innovation in economics. What began as a perk has turned into a parallel system of value, proving that even intangible rewards can hold tangible benefits — if you know how to use them. So the next time you board a plane, remember: you're not just flying; you're engaging in a micro-economy.

The Weimar Republic Hyperinflation

The economic collapse of post-World War I Germany is the stuff of financial nightmares. During the early 1920s, the Weimar Republic faced hyperinflation so severe that workers were paid twice a day to beat skyrocketing prices. Imagine cashing your paycheck in the morning and needing a wheelbarrow full of money for a loaf of bread by lunch.

Hyperinflation was fueled by reparations from the Treaty of Versailles and an overzealous printing press. The value of the German mark plummeted, and the government's solution—to print more money—only worsened the crisis. People burned banknotes for heat because it was cheaper than buying firewood. Meanwhile, artists and thinkers like Bertolt Brecht and Hannah Höch chronicled the chaos, capturing the surreal disarray of the times.

The collapse of the mark left an indelible mark on Germany's psyche, paving the way for political and economic shifts that would alter history. It's a stark reminder of how quickly monetary systems can spiral out of control—and why wheelbarrows are better suited for gardening than grocery shopping.

Whiskey as Legal Tender in Appalachia

In the rugged early days of the American frontier, when currency was scarce and banks were as reliable as a three-legged stool, whiskey emerged as a practical form of legal tender. Appalachia, with its plentiful corn and penchant for distilling, became a hotbed of booze-based economics.

Farmers used whiskey not just for drinking but for bartering. Need a new plow? That'll be two jugs of moonshine. The government even got in on the action by taxing distilled spirits, which sparked the infamous Whiskey Rebellion of 1794—a spirited protest, if there ever was one.

While the days of whiskey as currency are long gone, its legacy lingers in the region's culture. It's a reminder that when money's in short supply, ingenuity can turn even a stiff drink into cold, hard cash.

The Rise and Fall of the South Sea Bubble

In 1720, Britain experienced one of the first major stock market crashes, fueled by speculation over the South Sea Company. This firm promised enormous profits from trade in South America—despite having no actual trading rights. Investors flocked to buy shares, sending prices soaring.

As rumors of boundless riches spread, the bubble grew. Politicians, merchants, and even the King were caught in the frenzy. But when reality set in, the company's lack of actual assets became clear, and the bubble burst. Fortunes vanished overnight, leaving many in financial ruin.

The South Sea Bubble is a cautionary tale about the dangers of hype and herd mentality. It's a reminder that if an investment sounds too good to be true, it probably is—especially when the company you're betting on doesn't actually do anything.

The Lobster Was Once Peasant Food

Believe it or not, lobster wasn't always the overpriced delicacy we crack open at fancy dinners. In colonial America, it was so abundant that it washed ashore in piles, earning a reputation as "the cockroach of the sea." It was fed to prisoners, indentured servants, and even pigs.

Lobster's transformation began in the 19th century when canning technology made it a staple for urban workers. Later, railroads introduced it to inland diners as a luxury item. By the mid-20th century, clever marketing and scarcity elevated lobster to its current status as a gourmet treat.

The story of lobster is a delicious case of rags-to-riches, proving that with the right branding, even a sea bug can climb the social ladder. And it's a reminder that luxury is often a matter of perception—though you'll still need a second mortgage to enjoy it at a five-star restaurant.

Negative Interest Rates

Negative interest rates sound like economic science fiction, but they're very real. In times of economic downturn, central banks in countries like Japan and Switzerland have implemented this strategy to encourage borrowing and spending. Essentially, banks pay borrowers to take loans, turning traditional financial logic upside down.

The idea is to stimulate growth by making saving unattractive and borrowing irresistible. But it creates bizarre scenarios, like getting paid to hold a mortgage or earning less money by leaving it in the bank. Economists debate its long-term efficacy, with some calling it a clever tool and others dubbing it an economic Hail Mary.

Negative interest rates highlight the creativity—and occasional absurdity—of monetary policy. They're a reminder that in the world of economics, even the strangest ideas can become reality when the stakes are high enough. Just don't expect your savings account to thank you.

The Gold Rush and Levi's Jeans

The California Gold Rush of 1849 wasn't just about striking it rich with gold nuggets—it also paved the way for one of the most enduring fashion staples in history: Levi's jeans. As prospectors swarmed the rugged terrain in search of fortune, their flimsy trousers couldn't withstand the harsh conditions of mining. Enter Levi Strauss, a savvy German immigrant, who teamed up with tailor Jacob Davis to create sturdy work pants reinforced with copper rivets.

These pants, made from durable denim, quickly became a hit among miners, who appreciated their toughness and practicality. Originally called "waist overalls," Levi's jeans were the solution to back-breaking work in rough environments. Who knew that gold miners would kick off a fashion revolution?

Levi's jeans are now a global icon, worn by everyone from ranch hands to rock stars. Ironically, while many miners left the Gold Rush empty-handed, Strauss struck gold with denim, proving that sometimes the real treasure lies in meeting people's needs—not in a riverbed.

The Tulip Craze of Kazakhstan

Think tulip mania was exclusive to 17th-century Holland? Think again. Kazakhstan, the flower's ancestral home, is capitalizing on its tulip roots in a modern-day floral renaissance. As the birthplace of wild tulips, the country boasts stunning fields of vibrant blooms that have inspired a frenzy of tourism and scientific interest.

Kazakhstan has embraced the tulip as a national symbol, celebrating its heritage with festivals and conservation efforts. Unlike the Dutch mania, this modern craze focuses less on speculation and more on appreciation of nature's beauty. Visitors flock to the steppe in spring, where wild tulips bloom in spectacular colors, creating an Instagram-worthy paradise.

The tulip craze in Kazakhstan proves that history and nature can come together to create economic and cultural blooms, no speculation required.

The "Haircut" Economy of Greece

During Greece's economic crisis in the 2010s, austerity measures forced many citizens to think outside the box—or in this case, the barbershop. With cash in short supply, Greeks turned to bartering, and haircuts became one of the hottest commodities. Need some vegetables? Trade a trim. Looking for plumbing services? Offer a snazzy new style.

The haircut economy reflected the resilience of Greek communities. People relied on their skills and services to keep life moving, fostering a spirit of cooperation and ingenuity. This informal system wasn't just about survival; it was about solidarity during tough times.

While Greece has since stabilized, the haircut economy remains a humorous and poignant reminder that when money dries up, creativity grows. After all, you can't print euros, but you can always snip and style.

The Sardine Economy of Portugal

In Portugal, sardines are more than just a snack—they're an economic and cultural institution. These tiny fish have been a staple of Portuguese cuisine for centuries, appearing in everything from traditional festivals to gourmet menus. But sardines aren't just delicious; they're a big business.

Fishing, canning, and exporting sardines have long supported coastal communities, driving both local economies and international trade. Today, sardines are also a major tourist attraction, with colorful cans becoming sought-after souvenirs. Lisbon even hosts a festival in honor of St. Anthony, where sardines grilled on open flames take center stage.

The sardine economy is a lesson in how even the smallest things can make a big splash. In Portugal, these humble fish are proof that sometimes, the best things really do come in small packages — or tins.

The Bartering Boom in Post-Soviet Russia

After the Soviet Union collapsed in 1991, cash became scarce in Russia, leading to a resurgence of bartering. Factories, farmers, and families exchanged goods and services to survive the economic chaos. Need groceries? Trade some machinery parts. Can't pay your workers? Give them sausages instead of rubles.

Bartering wasn't just about necessity — it became a way to keep the economy moving when traditional systems failed. Large companies even bartered for big-ticket items like oil and steel, creating a surreal mix of modern industry and medieval trade.

The bartering boom highlighted the resilience of the Russian people. Faced with unprecedented challenges, they found creative ways to adapt. While bartering has largely faded, it remains a fascinating chapter in the story of how societies cope when the wheels of commerce grind to a halt. It's also a reminder that, sometimes, sausages are worth their weight in gold.

Medical Madness

The Dancing Plague of 1518

In July 1518, the streets of Strasbourg were overtaken by a bizarre and deadly phenomenon: people dancing uncontrollably, seemingly against their will. What began with one woman twirling in the square soon grew to dozens, then hundreds, of citizens caught in the grip of a mysterious "dancing plague." They danced for days, collapsing from exhaustion, strokes, or even death, all while music was inexplicably played to encourage the movement.

Historians have debated the cause of this peculiar outbreak. Some blame ergot poisoning, a hallucinogenic mold found in rye bread. Others suggest mass hysteria, triggered by stress and social pressures of the time. Whatever the reason, the spectacle became a grim reminder of how the human mind and body can conspire in the most surreal ways.

The dancing plague has since become a symbol of unexplained mass behaviors, though today's equivalent might involve going viral on TikTok—thankfully with less fatal consequences.

The Surgeon Who Operated on Himself

In 1961, Dr. Leonid Rogozov found himself in the most literal definition of self-care. Stationed in Antarctica with a Soviet research team, he developed appendicitis. The problem? No other surgeon was within 1,000 miles, and the worsening infection was life-threatening.

So, Rogozov did what few could imagine—he performed an appendectomy on himself. With a mirror and the assistance of his colleagues (who were more moral support than medical help), Rogozov removed his appendix in a two-hour ordeal. He paused occasionally to catch his breath and mop his brow, but against all odds, he succeeded and recovered fully.

Rogozov's feat remains a testament to human determination and grit, proving that sometimes, when no one else can save you, you simply have to grab the scalpel yourself.

The Radium Girls

In the early 1900s, young women working in factories were tasked with painting watch dials with glow-in-the-dark radium paint. They were instructed to use their lips to shape the paintbrushes into fine points, unknowingly ingesting radium with each stroke. Dubbed the "Radium Girls," these workers began to suffer horrific effects: brittle bones, severe anemia, and in some cases, their jaws literally disintegrated.

At the time, radium was marketed as a miracle substance, even added to toothpaste and cosmetics. The Radium Girls' plight eventually led to lawsuits, raising awareness about occupational safety and sparking reforms that protected future workers.

Their tragic story is a chilling reminder of the cost of progress, where innovation outpaced understanding, leaving these women to pay the ultimate price.

The Man with the Iron Stomach

Alexis St. Martin, a fur trader in 1820s Canada, gained unexpected fame when a shotgun blast left him with a hole in his stomach. Enter Dr. William Beaumont, a curious physician who saw the wound not as a tragedy but as a once-in-a-lifetime research opportunity.

Using the open wound, Beaumont conducted experiments on digestion, lowering food directly into St. Martin's stomach and observing the process. Though ethically dubious, his work laid the foundation for modern gastroenterology. St. Martin endured years of being poked and prodded, possibly fueled by equal parts necessity and curiosity.

The man with the iron stomach not only survived but became a medical marvel. His unique case proved that science sometimes progresses in the strangest—and messiest—ways.

The Plague Doctor's Beak Mask

The iconic plague doctor's mask, with its long, bird-like beak, is the stuff of medieval nightmares. Worn by physicians during the Black Death, the mask was designed to protect the wearer from "miasma," or bad air, which was believed to carry disease. The beak was filled with herbs, spices, and flowers to mask the stench and, supposedly, to ward off illness.

While the intent was noble, the masks were woefully ineffective. The real plague carriers were fleas and rats, which no amount of perfumed rosemary could deter. However, the eerie ensemble did leave a lasting impression, cementing the image of the beaked plague doctor in popular culture.

Today, the mask stands as a symbol of both the ingenuity and the ignorance of the time—a reminder that even the creepiest designs are born of desperate attempts to solve life-or-death problems.

The Case of Phineas Gage

Phineas Gage was a mild-mannered railroad worker until one fateful day in 1848 when an iron rod shot through his skull, making him the unintentional poster child for neuroscience. The rod entered below his left cheekbone and exited through the top of his head, leaving him very much alive—but profoundly changed.

Amazingly, Gage not only survived but became a walking case study for how the brain influences personality. Before the accident, he was known for his steady demeanor and responsible nature. Afterward, he became impulsive, irritable, and, some say, downright rude. His transformation intrigued scientists, proving for the first time that specific areas of the brain control behavior and personality.

Gage's story is both horrifying and fascinating, a tale of survival that paved the way for modern brain research. It's also a reminder to never underestimate the power of a really unlucky day on the job.

The Use of Leeches in Medicine

Leeches have been slithering their way into medical history for centuries, and surprisingly, they're still around. While medieval doctors used them to "balance humors" (translation: bloodletting for just about any ailment), today's doctors employ these slimy creatures for more precise purposes.

Leeches are used in modern surgeries to restore circulation in reattached fingers and other delicate procedures. Their saliva contains anticoagulants that prevent clotting, making them tiny, natural blood thinners. It's like having a squirmy little surgeon that works for blood.

The next time you're grossed out by leeches, remember they might be life-saving medical heroes. Just don't expect them to smile for the camera—they're not that kind of team player.

The First Face Transplant

In 2005, a groundbreaking medical feat stunned the world: the first partial face transplant. Isabelle Dinoire, a Frenchwoman disfigured by a dog attack, received a new nose, lips, and chin from a deceased donor. The surgery was as complex ethically as it was surgically.

Doctors had to navigate not only the medical challenges of rejection and infection but also the psychological impact on the recipient. How do you adjust to looking in the mirror and seeing someone else's face—sort of? Dinoire herself described the emotional and physical hurdles she faced, including the lifelong need for immunosuppressant drugs.

The transplant opened doors for countless others suffering from severe facial injuries. It also raised profound questions about identity, beauty, and medical boundaries, proving that medicine's most miraculous achievements often come with layers of complexity.

Laughing Death: The Kuru Disease

"Kuru," or "laughing death," sounds like the title of a dark comedy, but it's a chilling disease that devastated the Fore people of Papua New Guinea. The fatal neurological disorder, first documented in the 1950s, caused uncontrollable laughter, tremors, and eventually death.

The cause? Cannibalistic rituals. The Fore practiced endocannibalism, consuming the brains of deceased loved ones as part of their mourning process. Unfortunately, this spread prions—infectious proteins that destroy brain tissue, leading to kuru.

Once the practice ended, so did the disease, but its eerie symptoms and tragic backstory remain a haunting example of how culture and biology can intersect in unexpected ways. It's a sobering reminder that not all traditions stand the test of time—especially the ones involving brain snacks.

The Woman Who Couldn't Feel Pain

Imagine going through life never feeling pain. Sounds great, right? For Jo Cameron, a Scottish woman with a rare genetic mutation, this is her reality—but it's not all superpowers and smiles.

Cameron's mutation prevents her from experiencing pain, anxiety, or stress. While this might sound like a dream come true, it comes with risks. She's broken bones without realizing it and required emergency surgeries for injuries that would have sent anyone else to the hospital long before.

Her condition has intrigued scientists, who hope to unlock new pain treatments by studying her unique genetic makeup. Cameron's story is a reminder that even what seems like a blessing can have its complications—and that pain, as much as we hate it, serves an important purpose in keeping us safe.

The Vampire Cure: Bloodletting

Once upon a time, if you felt under the weather, your doctor's solution might have been to let you bleed. Bloodletting, practiced for over 2,000 years, was based on the idea of balancing the body's "humors." Feeling feverish? Out with some blood. Acting a bit eccentric? Surely, your veins were to blame.

Even George Washington reportedly underwent bloodletting during his final illness, which likely didn't help matters.

The process ranged from leeches doing the dirty work to sharp tools that would make a modern surgeon faint. The practice reached absurd levels, with barbers doubling as bloodletters—a role immortalized by the red-and-white barber pole. Unfortunately, the "cure" often caused more harm than good, leaving patients weakened or even dead.

While bloodletting is now relegated to history (mostly), its bizarre reign reminds us how far medicine has come—and why you should be grateful for today's evidence-based treatments.

The Wandering Womb

If ancient Greek physicians were to be believed, a woman's uterus had a mind of its own, roaming around her body like a restless traveler. This "wandering womb" theory, popularized by Hippocrates, was thought to cause ailments ranging from hysteria to fainting.

The cure? Fragrant herbs or even unpleasant smells aimed at "luring" the womb back to its rightful place. Modern medicine, of course, has debunked this entirely, but the idea lingered for centuries, giving us terms like "hysteria," derived from the Greek word for uterus, hystera.

It's a laughable relic of history but also a sobering reminder of how misunderstandings about women's health have shaped (and hindered) medical progress. Thankfully, the womb no longer gets blamed for wandering off like a curious toddler.

The Boy Who Lived in a Bubble

David Vetter, known as "The Boy in the Bubble," was born in 1971 with severe combined immunodeficiency (SCID), a condition that left him with virtually no immune defenses. To keep him safe, doctors placed him in a sterile plastic bubble, where he spent most of his short life.

While the bubble protected David from infections, it isolated him from the outside world. He received schooling, toys, and even a specially designed "spacesuit" to explore beyond his enclosure. Despite these efforts, David yearned for normalcy, and his story became a poignant symbol of both scientific innovation and its limits.

David's legacy lives on through advancements in gene therapy and SCID treatments, ensuring others won't face life in a bubble. His story is both heartbreaking and inspiring—a testament to the resilience of the human spirit, even when confined by plastic walls.

The First X-Ray Accident

When Wilhelm Röntgen discovered X-rays in 1895, he probably didn't imagine they'd revolutionize medicine and accidentally harm their users. Early radiologists, fascinated by this new technology, eagerly exposed themselves to radiation without understanding its risks.

Thomas Edison's assistant, Clarence Dally, was one of the first to suffer. Constant exposure while experimenting with X-ray tubes caused severe burns, leading to amputations and eventually his death. These tragic incidents taught scientists about the dangers of radiation and spurred the development of protective measures like lead aprons.

The X-ray's early days were a mix of brilliance and recklessness, a time when progress sometimes came with literal burning questions. It's a cautionary tale about the price of discovery—and why you should thank your radiologist for their modern safety protocols.

The Use of Maggots in Modern Medicine

Maggots in medicine might sound like a medieval nightmare, but these wiggly creatures are making a comeback in modern wound care. Maggot therapy involves placing sterilized fly larvae on wounds to eat dead tissue, a process called debridement.

Despite their squirm-inducing reputation, maggots are remarkably effective. They clean wounds with precision, promoting faster healing and reducing the risk of infection. Their secret? A combination of enzymes and antibacterial properties that make them nature's tiny surgeons.

Maggot therapy is a reminder that sometimes, the grossest solutions are the most effective. It's proof that even the humblest creatures can play a role in modern medicine—just don't expect them to be invited to dinner.

The Birth of the Stethoscope

In 1816, Dr. René Laennec faced a dilemma: a young woman needed a chest examination, but pressing his ear against her chest (the standard practice of the time) felt a little too intimate. In a flash of modesty-fueled genius, Laennec rolled up a sheet of paper, creating a makeshift listening tube—and the stethoscope was born.

This simple invention revolutionized medicine. By amplifying internal sounds, the stethoscope allowed doctors to diagnose heart and lung conditions with unprecedented accuracy.

Laennec later refined his device, crafting a wooden version and documenting its use in a groundbreaking treatise.

Today, the stethoscope remains a symbol of medicine, though it's gone high-tech with electronic models and Bluetooth capabilities. It's a reminder that innovation often springs from unexpected moments — and that modesty can sometimes change the world.

The Unethical Tuskegee Syphilis Study

From 1932 to 1972, one of the darkest chapters in medical history unfolded in Tuskegee, Alabama. The Tuskegee Syphilis Study involved hundreds of African American men who were misled into believing they were receiving treatment for syphilis. In reality, researchers withheld treatment to study the disease's progression.

The men suffered severe health consequences, and many died as a result. The study wasn't just unethical — it was a betrayal of trust that reverberates to this day, influencing attitudes toward medical institutions and highlighting systemic racism in healthcare.

The scandal led to stricter ethical guidelines for research, including the requirement of informed consent. It's a grim reminder of the importance of accountability in science — and the cost of its absence.

The Elephant Man's Condition

Joseph Merrick, known as the "Elephant Man," captivated Victorian society with his extreme deformities. Born in 1862, Merrick suffered from a combination of conditions, possibly Proteus syndrome or neurofibromatosis, which caused abnormal growths and disfigurements.

Despite being exhibited as a sideshow curiosity, Merrick's intelligence and humanity shone through. He eventually found refuge at London Hospital, where he formed a close friendship with Dr. Frederick Treves. Merrick's life remains a poignant exploration of compassion and the societal treatment of those who look different.

Merrick's story is a reminder that behind every medical mystery is a person with hopes, struggles, and dignity—a lesson as relevant now as it was in his time.

The Mystery of Spontaneous Human Combustion

Few phenomena are as chilling—literally—as spontaneous human combustion (SHC). Reports of people mysteriously bursting into flames, leaving behind only charred remains and unscathed surroundings, have baffled scientists and fueled wild theories.

Skeptics attribute SHC to mundane causes, like a dropped cigarette igniting clothing, exacerbated by the "wick effect," where body fat acts like candle wax. True believers, however, propose everything from alcohol saturation to supernatural forces.

While SHC remains largely debunked, it's a macabre curiosity that taps into our fear of the inexplicable. Whether science or mystery, it's a fiery topic that refuses to be extinguished.

The Discovery of Penicillin

Alexander Fleming's discovery of penicillin in 1928 was, quite literally, a happy accident. Returning to his lab after a vacation, Fleming noticed a mold (later identified as Penicillium notatum) killing bacteria on a forgotten petri dish. Realizing its potential, he began the journey toward creating the first antibiotic.

Penicillin transformed medicine, saving countless lives by treating infections that were once death sentences. Its impact during World War II was monumental, helping wounded soldiers recover and underscoring the importance of scientific innovation.

Fleming's breakthrough reminds us that even in the messiness of life—or a cluttered lab—world-changing discoveries can emerge. Sometimes, all it takes is a sharp eye, an open mind, and a little moldy luck.

Astronomical Oddities

The Hexagonal Storm on Saturn

Saturn, the gas giant with those iconic rings, has another mesmerizing feature: a six-sided storm at its north pole. Discovered by the Voyager spacecraft in the 1980s and later captured in stunning detail by Cassini, this hexagonal hurricane spans over 20,000 miles and boasts wind speeds of 200 mph. But what's most baffling is its near-perfect geometric shape—how does a planet whip up a storm that would make a geometry teacher swoon?

Scientists believe the hexagon's shape is caused by jet streams and differences in atmospheric rotation. Think of it like swirling cream in your coffee—if your barista were a planetary giant with a knack for symmetry. Yet, despite extensive modeling, the exact mechanics remain a puzzle, leaving room for plenty of speculation (and sci-fi-worthy theories).

Saturn's hexagon reminds us that nature doesn't just create beauty—it can do so with mathematical precision. It's the ultimate cosmic flex, proving that even storms can think outside the box—or inside the hexagon.

The Black Hole That's "Burping" Gas

Black holes are infamous for consuming everything in their vicinity, but did you know they sometimes "burp"? In a galaxy 800 million light-years away, a supermassive black hole has been observed ejecting massive bursts of gas. This cosmic indigestion occurs when a black hole gobbles up too much matter, expelling some of it back into space at mind-blowing speeds.

Astronomers have likened this phenomenon to a black hole eating too quickly and needing to let off steam. These gas outflows can shape entire galaxies, triggering star formation or, paradoxically, halting it. It's like the ultimate cosmic recycling program—if your recycling bin also obliterated everything in its path.

This burping black hole challenges our understanding of these celestial beasts, proving they're not just bottomless pits but dynamic, active players in the universe's evolution. Even in the vastness of space, it seems no one escapes the occasional hiccup.

The Star That's a Giant Diamond

Some stars go out in a blaze of glory, but not "Lucy." This white dwarf, located 50 light-years from Earth, has crystallized into a diamond roughly the size of our Moon. Composed primarily of carbon, it's estimated to weigh an unimaginable 10 billion trillion carats, making it the largest cosmic gemstone in existence.

Astronomers named it after the Beatles' song "Lucy in the Sky with Diamonds," because what else do you call a star that's literally sparkling? One day, billions of years from now, our Sun might undergo a similar transformation, leaving a diamond legacy of its own.

Lucy is a reminder that the universe has a flair for drama and beauty, even in death. So the next time someone brags about their jewelry, just mention the giant diamond in space—they'll have nothing to top that.

The Planet That Rains Glass Sideways

HD 189733b might sound like a robot's serial number, but it's actually one of the most terrifying planets discovered outside our solar system. Located 63 light-years away, this exoplanet is a study in extremes. Its winds reach speeds of 5,400 mph, and its skies rain molten glass—sideways.

The planet's blue hue, reminiscent of Earth, is caused by silicate particles in its atmosphere, which scatter light. But don't let the pretty color fool you—HD 189733b is essentially the universe's version of a glassblowing studio gone rogue.

While it's not a place for intergalactic tourism, this hellish world offers valuable insights into the diversity of exoplanets and their atmospheres. It's a cosmic reminder that beauty and danger often go hand in hand—or, in this case, sideways.

The Coldest Place in the Universe

If you thought Antarctica was chilly, meet the Boomerang Nebula. Located 5,000 light-years away, this dying star's outer layers are expanding so rapidly that its temperature has plummeted to -457.7°F—colder than the background radiation left over from the Big Bang.

The nebula's frigid temperatures are caused by its rapid expansion, which cools the gas to almost absolute zero. It's like the universe's version of flash-freezing, except instead of preserving peas, it's sculpting a cosmic ice sculpture.

The Boomerang Nebula stands as a testament to the universe's ability to surprise us with extremes. Whether it's fiery stars or frozen nebulas, space continues to show that it doesn't do anything halfway—and it never forgets its cool factor.

Rogue Planets Drifting Through Space

Imagine a planet without a star to call home, floating alone in the vast emptiness of space. These are rogue planets, celestial wanderers unbound by the gravitational pull of a star. They roam freely across the galaxy, untethered and mysterious, like cosmic orphans in the coldest and darkest of voids.

Scientists believe these planets form like regular planets but are ejected from their solar systems due to gravitational interactions. Some may have been flung into space during violent cosmic events, while others might have formed in isolation. Without a star to provide light and warmth, rogue planets are shrouded in eternal night, making them exceptionally difficult to study.

These nomadic worlds raise fascinating questions: Could they harbor life deep below their surfaces, warmed by internal heat? Or are they barren, frozen wastelands? The possibilities make them the ultimate cosmic enigma, proving that even in the vastness of space, there's room for a little mystery.

The Pulsar Lighthouse Effect

Neutron stars, the dense remnants of supernova explosions, are among the universe's most fascinating objects. But when they spin rapidly and emit beams of radiation from their magnetic poles, they create a phenomenon known as the "pulsar lighthouse effect."

As the neutron star rotates, its beams sweep across the cosmos like a lighthouse, creating flashes of light visible from Earth at precise intervals. These pulses are so regular that pulsars were initially mistaken for signals from extraterrestrial life — scientists even nicknamed the first one "LGM-1" (for "Little Green Men").

Pulsars serve as natural cosmic clocks, helping astronomers study everything from the behavior of matter under extreme gravity to the distribution of galaxies. They're a reminder that even the aftermath of a stellar death can create something wondrous—and a bit hypnotic.

The Great Attractor's Gravitational Mystery

Deep in the universe, something massive and unseen exerts a gravitational pull so strong it's dragging entire galaxy clusters toward it, including our own Milky Way. This mysterious force is known as the Great Attractor, and its true nature remains one of astronomy's great puzzles.

The Great Attractor is located in a region of space obscured by the Milky Way's dense dust and gas, making it frustratingly difficult to study. Scientists speculate it could be a supercluster of galaxies, a massive black hole, or even evidence of dark matter. Whatever it is, its pull is immense, shaping the motion of galaxies over hundreds of millions of light-years.

This gravitational enigma reminds us that the universe is full of hidden wonders. While we might not fully understand the Great Attractor, its existence is a cosmic breadcrumb, leading us closer to the mysteries of the universe's invisible forces.

The Darkest Known Planet

TrES-2b, an exoplanet orbiting a star 750 light-years away, holds the title of the darkest known planet. This alien world absorbs 99% of the light that hits it, making it appear pitch black—darker than coal or black acrylic paint.

What makes TrES-2b so dark? Scientists believe its atmosphere, filled with light-absorbing chemicals like vaporized sodium and potassium, traps nearly all incoming light. It's the ultimate cosmic black hole for photons, though it still emits a faint red glow from its extreme heat.

Despite its darkness, TrES-2b is a shining example of the universe's diversity. It's a reminder that even in the vastness of space, the most unexpected and extreme phenomena are waiting to be discovered—just don't expect it to brighten your day.

The Fastest Spinning Star

Meet VFTS 102, a star in the Tarantula Nebula spinning at a staggering 1 million miles per hour. This cosmic speedster is so fast that it's nearly tearing itself apart, with centrifugal forces pushing its surface outward.

Scientists believe VFTS 102's incredible velocity could be the result of a close encounter with a binary partner or a nearby supernova, which gave it a literal spin boost. Its rapid rotation has flattened it into an oblate shape, making it look less like a perfect sphere and more like a cosmic pancake.

VFTS 102 is a stellar daredevil, living on the edge of self-destruction. It's a fascinating reminder of the extremes that stars can reach and a testament to the relentless energy of the universe—always spinning, always dazzling, always surprising.

The Planet That Orbits Its Star Backward

WASP-17b is the rebellious teenager of the exoplanet world, defying expectations by orbiting its star in the "wrong" direction. Unlike most planets, which follow the same rotational direction as their stars, WASP-17b moves in a retrograde orbit—essentially backward in astronomical terms. This bizarre behavior has scientists scratching their heads.

The leading theory is that a gravitational interaction with another celestial body, possibly a nearby massive planet or star, disrupted WASP-17b's orbit early in its formation. The result is a cosmic dance partner spinning to its own rhythm, proving that even planets can have attitude.

This anomaly challenges our understanding of planetary formation and dynamics. WASP-17b is a reminder that space, like life, loves to throw curveballs, and sometimes the most interesting things happen when something doesn't follow the rules.

The Galactic Wall

The Galactic Wall, also known as the Hercules-Corona Borealis Great Wall, is the cosmic equivalent of discovering the Great Wall of China but on a mind-boggling scale. This colossal structure, composed of interconnected galaxies, stretches over a billion light-years and is one of the largest known formations in the universe.

Its sheer size challenges existing models of cosmic structure and the uniformity of the universe. How did such a massive entity come to exist? Gravity is the primary suspect, pulling galaxies into these interconnected chains over billions of years.

The Galactic Wall is a humbling reminder of just how small we are in the cosmic scheme. While it's unlikely we'll ever visit, it's nice to know that even the universe can't resist building something awe-inspiringly massive.

The Hypervelocity Stars

Imagine being a star hurtling through space at over 1 million miles per hour. That's the reality for hypervelocity stars, celestial bodies ejected from galaxies at incredible speeds. These runaway stars are typically flung out by interactions with black holes, which act as cosmic slingshots.

The most common scenario involves a binary star system venturing too close to a black hole. One star is captured, while the other is sent flying at breakneck speed, like a pinball in a cosmic arcade. These stars are so fast that they can escape their home galaxies entirely, becoming intergalactic wanderers.

Hypervelocity stars are a testament to the chaotic and violent nature of the cosmos. They're also a reminder that in space, as in life, the right nudge—or wrong one—can send you soaring into the unknown.

The Largest Known Explosion

In 2008, astronomers observed an explosion so immense it defies comprehension. The gamma-ray burst GRB 080916C released more energy in 10 seconds than our Sun will produce over its entire 10-billion-year lifespan. Located 12.2 billion light-years away, this burst was the death cry of a collapsing star turning into a black hole.

Gamma-ray bursts are the most powerful explosions in the universe, emitting jets of high-energy radiation. GRB 080916C was a standout due to its extraordinary intensity and the speed of its particles, which neared the speed of light.

This cosmic firework reminds us of the sheer power and drama of the universe. It's a stark contrast to our relatively calm solar system and a reminder that somewhere out there, the cosmos is throwing parties on a scale we can barely fathom.

The Loneliest Galaxy

MCG+01-02-015 is the loneliest galaxy in the known universe, a cosmic introvert sitting 100 million light-years from its nearest neighbor. In a universe filled with bustling clusters and interactions, this galaxy exists in isolation, floating in a vast expanse of emptiness known as the cosmic void.

Astronomers believe its solitude is due to its location in a sparsely populated region of space, where galaxy formation was minimal. Its isolation offers unique opportunities to study galactic evolution without the interference of neighbors.

The Loneliest Galaxy is a poignant reminder that even in the vast, crowded universe, some entities exist entirely on their own. Its solitude, however, gives it a quiet kind of beauty — a cosmic lighthouse standing resolute in the void.

Zombie Stars

Zombie stars are the universe's undead, white dwarfs that come back to life by siphoning material from a companion star. These remnants of once-luminous stars quietly orbit their partners, gathering stolen hydrogen and helium like cosmic vampires. When their stolen bounty reaches a tipping point, the star reignites in a thermonuclear explosion — a Type Ia supernova.

These stellar detonations are a big deal, not just because they're visually stunning, but because they serve as "standard candles" for astronomers. Since these explosions always produce a consistent brightness, they help scientists measure distances across the universe. Ironically, these undead stars are instrumental in understanding the living universe.

Zombie stars remind us that in space, as in horror movies, sometimes the dead don't stay dead. And when they do rise again, they go out with an unforgettable bang.

Quasars: The Bright Beacons of the Universe

Quasars are the universe's disco balls—if disco balls were powered by black holes. These brilliant objects are found at the centers of active galaxies, where supermassive black holes devour matter at astonishing rates. The resulting friction generates energy so intense that a single quasar can outshine entire galaxies.

First discovered in the 1960s, quasars were initially mistaken for stars due to their incredible luminosity. However, they're anything but ordinary. Their light has traveled billions of years to reach us, offering a glimpse into the early universe.

Quasars are a testament to cosmic extremes, where destruction and creation coexist in dazzling harmony. They're the ultimate light show—on a galactic scale.

The Interstellar Visitor: 'Oumuamua

In 2017, something strange zipped through our solar system—a cigar-shaped object named 'Oumuamua, meaning "scout" in Hawaiian. Unlike anything seen before, this interstellar visitor traveled too fast to be bound by the Sun's gravity, marking it as a traveler from another star system.

Scientists debated its origins. Was it an asteroid? A comet? Or, as some suggested, an alien probe? 'Oumuamua's odd shape and lack of a comet-like tail fueled speculation, making it one of astronomy's greatest mysteries.

While the alien theory remains unlikely, 'Oumuamua is a cosmic reminder of how little we know about the universe. It's a brief, enigmatic postcard from the stars, inviting us to keep looking up—and wondering.

The Dark Energy Mystery

Dark energy is the cosmic equivalent of an unexplained speeding ticket. This mysterious force, which makes up 68% of the universe, is driving the accelerated expansion of space itself. First discovered in the late 1990s, dark energy has left scientists scratching their heads ever since.

Theories abound, from the energy of empty space to an entirely new physics we haven't yet grasped. Whatever it is, dark energy is shaping the fate of the universe, potentially stretching it to a cold, lonely "Big Freeze."

The mystery of dark energy underscores how much we still don't understand about the cosmos. It's a humbling reminder that for all our advancements, the universe keeps its biggest secrets close.

The Moon That Shouldn't Exist

Saturn's moon Enceladus is a tiny, icy orb that defies expectations. Beneath its frozen crust lies a global subsurface ocean, kept warm by tidal forces from Saturn's gravity. To top it off, Enceladus spews massive geysers of water vapor and ice particles into space, creating a stunning display and feeding Saturn's E-ring.

What makes Enceladus so intriguing is its potential for life. Where there's water, heat, and organic compounds — as detected in its geysers — there could be microbes or more. For a moon barely 300 miles across, Enceladus punches far above its weight in scientific fascination.

Enceladus is a cosmic underdog, a tiny moon with a big story. It reminds us that sometimes, the smallest worlds hold the biggest surprises — and the promise of life beyond Earth.

Technological Marvels

The Internet's Origin as ARPANET

Long before the internet turned into a place for memes, cat videos, and heated online debates, it had humble beginnings as ARPANET—a U.S. government project in the late 1960s. The goal was to create a communication system that would allow researchers at different universities to share data efficiently, even during a nuclear crisis. Not exactly the kind of thing you'd expect to lead to TikTok, but here we are.

The first message sent over ARPANET on October 29, 1969, was supposed to be "LOGIN," but the system crashed after "LO." (Even the early internet struggled with glitches.) Yet, ARPANET kept evolving, connecting more nodes and eventually giving rise to the protocols that form the backbone of today's World Wide Web.

From its nerdy research roots, ARPANET blossomed into a global phenomenon, proving that even the most serious projects can lead to surprising and transformative outcomes. Today, we owe everything from online shopping to endlessly streaming shows to this unlikely origin story.

The Fax Machine Predates the Telephone

Surprise! The fax machine is the elder statesman of communication technology, predating the telephone by over 30 years. Scottish inventor Alexander Bain developed the first fax-like device in the 1840s, capable of sending images over telegraph wires. Imagine the reaction back then: "You're telling me you can send a picture through a wire? Witchcraft!"

The technology slowly evolved, finding its heyday in the late 20th century. By then, fax machines became staples of offices worldwide, delivering blurry but legible documents in minutes. Now, in the digital age, fax machines have mostly retired, though they still haunt doctor's offices and government forms.

So the next time someone calls a fax machine outdated, remind them it was revolutionizing communication while the telephone was just a twinkle in Alexander Graham Bell's eye.

The Great Pacific Garbage Patch Cleanup

Imagine a swirling island of trash twice the size of Texas, floating in the Pacific Ocean. This isn't the plot of a dystopian sci-fi film — it's the Great Pacific Garbage Patch, a grim reminder of humanity's waste problem. But hope floats, literally, thanks to innovative cleanup technology.

The Ocean Cleanup, a non-profit organization, is tackling the patch with a fleet of autonomous systems designed to trap plastic waste without harming marine life. Since launching in 2013, they've collected thousands of tons of trash, proving that big problems require bold solutions.

While there's still a long way to go, the cleanup effort shows that technology and environmentalism can team up to tackle even the messiest challenges. Who knew saving the planet could start with a giant trash net?

The Rise of 3D Printing

3D printing is like something out of a sci-fi movie: machines that can create objects layer by layer from digital designs. Initially used for prototyping in the 1980s, the technology has exploded into everyday life, producing everything from prosthetic limbs to entire houses. Yes, houses.

The secret lies in its versatility. 3D printers can use materials ranging from plastics to metals and even food. Want a custom chocolate sculpture? There's a printer for that. Need an organ transplant? Researchers are working on bio-printing human tissue.

3D printing is democratizing manufacturing, allowing anyone with a design and a printer to become a maker. It's not just a technological leap—it's a creative revolution.

The Voyager Golden Record

In 1977, NASA launched the Voyager spacecraft to explore the far reaches of the solar system. Aboard each probe was the Golden Record, a phonograph containing sounds, music, and images from Earth—a cosmic mixtape for alien civilizations.

Curated by a team led by Carl Sagan, the record features everything from Beethoven and Chuck Berry to greetings in 55 languages and the sound of a baby crying. If aliens find it, they'll know we're a species that loves variety—and occasionally loses sleep.

The Golden Record is a beautiful reminder of humanity's curiosity and optimism. It's our way of saying, "Hey, universe! We're here, and we have some pretty good tunes."

The Hadron Collider's Particle Quest

Buried deep beneath the border of France and Switzerland lies a 17-mile-long circular tunnel that houses the Large Hadron Collider (LHC) — the world's most powerful particle accelerator. This marvel of modern science isn't just a massive underground racetrack for protons; it's a gateway to understanding the fundamental building blocks of the universe.

The LHC made headlines in 2012 when it helped scientists discover the elusive Higgs boson, often dubbed the "God Particle." This discovery confirmed theories about how particles gain mass, fundamentally shaping our understanding of physics. But don't let the nickname fool you — the Higgs boson isn't about divinity; it's about deciphering the universe's most intricate secrets.

Though the LHC sounds intimidating, it's also a triumph of human curiosity and collaboration. Thousands of scientists work together, smashing particles at nearly the speed of light to unlock the universe's deepest mysteries. It's science at its most explosive — literally.

The Artificial Intelligence That Defeated Chess Masters

In 1997, IBM's Deep Blue made history by defeating world chess champion Garry Kasparov. This wasn't just a victory for AI; it was a seismic moment in our relationship with technology. Suddenly, machines weren't just tools — they could outthink us in complex strategy games.

Deep Blue's victory marked the dawn of modern AI, paving the way for smarter, more adaptive systems. Today, algorithms like AlphaZero don't just play chess — they dominate it, learning strategies independently. Meanwhile, we humans cling to our checkmate dreams, now and forever outclassed.

AI's triumph in chess symbolizes more than just computing power; it's a reflection of how technology reshapes human potential—and keeps us humble.

The Mars Rover's Epic Adventures

When the Mars rover Curiosity touched down in 2012, it carried humanity's hopes for understanding the Red Planet. Since then, it has explored Martian terrain, drilled into rocks, and even sang "Happy Birthday" to itself—making it arguably the loneliest birthday bash in the solar system.

Curiosity's success inspired Perseverance, the rover that landed in 2021. Equipped with advanced tools, including a helicopter named Ingenuity, Perseverance is searching for signs of ancient life. Each image and data packet it sends back feels like a postcard from a distant world.

Mars rovers are the embodiment of human ingenuity and exploration. They're our robotic ambassadors, turning a barren planet into a treasure trove of discovery, one dusty wheelprint at a time.

The Rise and Fall of Google Glass

In 2013, Google Glass burst onto the scene as a glimpse into a sci-fi future: augmented reality glasses that could display notifications, record videos, and make you look like a tech-savvy cyborg. But instead of changing the world, it mostly earned raised eyebrows and privacy concerns.

Google Glass flopped commercially, criticized for being expensive and, well, a little creepy. Still, it laid the groundwork for future innovations in augmented reality, influencing industries from healthcare to entertainment.

Sometimes, even the tech world needs a beta test—and Google Glass, for all its flaws, was a bold step toward the future.

The World's First Robot Citizen

In 2017, Saudi Arabia made headlines by granting citizenship to Sophia, a humanoid robot powered by artificial intelligence. With lifelike expressions and an eerily human voice, Sophia stirred equal parts wonder and unease. Was this a glimpse into a robotic future—or the beginning of a sci-fi dystopia?

Sophia's creators intended her to promote AI's potential to solve global challenges. She's participated in interviews, even cracking jokes, but skeptics argue her "intelligence" is largely scripted—a performance, not true sentience.

Robot citizenship raises fascinating questions about identity, rights, and ethics. For now, Sophia is more symbol than substance, but she reminds us that the future is closer—and stranger—than we think.

The Technology Behind Self-Driving Cars

Self-driving cars sound like the stuff of sci-fi, but thanks to AI, they're quickly becoming a reality. These vehicles combine sensors, cameras, radar, and advanced algorithms to navigate roads, avoid obstacles, and make split-second decisions—all without a human at the wheel. It's like giving your car a brain and then nervously hoping it doesn't daydream at a green light.

The magic lies in machine learning, where cars are trained on countless scenarios to understand road behavior. Sensors detect surroundings in real-time, creating a 360-degree awareness that even the best drivers can't match. Still, self-driving cars face challenges, from interpreting tricky traffic situations to managing unpredictable human drivers (we see you, left-lane hogs).

While the tech isn't perfect yet, it promises a future of fewer accidents, smoother commutes, and the luxury of scrolling through your phone guilt-free—legally, this time.

The Floating Solar Farms

When land is scarce and energy demands are high, why not take to the water? Floating solar farms are doing just that, turning lakes, reservoirs, and even oceans into renewable energy hotspots. These solar panels float atop water, reducing evaporation and generating electricity at the same time.

Not only do they save space, but their watery homes keep them cool, boosting efficiency. Countries like China, Japan, and India have already adopted this technology, transforming quiet lakes into powerhouses of sustainability.

Floating solar farms are proof that innovation floats—not just on ideas, but literally on water.

The Smart Contact Lenses of the Future

Imagine contact lenses that double as augmented reality (AR) displays or mini health monitors. These sci-fi-worthy smart lenses are being developed to project data directly into your field of vision, turning your eyes into high-tech HUDs (Heads-Up Displays).

Future lenses might help diabetics monitor glucose levels or alert users to allergens in the air. Meanwhile, AR applications could let you check emails, directions, or even translate signs in real-time—all without reaching for a screen. Goodbye, clunky glasses; hello, cyberpunk chic.

As groundbreaking as they are, smart lenses will have their challenges—like not losing them in the sink. Still, they're a small step for contact lenses, but a giant leap for tech-savvy eyeballs.

Blockchain Beyond Cryptocurrency

Blockchain may have started as the backbone of Bitcoin, but its uses go far beyond cryptocurrency. At its core, blockchain is a decentralized, tamper-proof ledger—a digital system for recording data in a way that's transparent and secure.

From secure online voting to tracking food origins in supply chains, blockchain is revolutionizing industries by ensuring trust and accountability. In healthcare, it's being used to store patient records securely, while in the art world, it verifies digital ownership of NFTs.

Though blockchain has its critics—looking at you, environmentalists concerned about energy use—it's a game-changer for systems that rely on transparency. It's like the internet got an upgrade, but instead of cat videos, it's delivering trust.

The Space Elevator Concept

Picture an elevator stretching from Earth to space—a tethered structure that could transport goods and people without rockets. The concept of a space elevator has fascinated scientists for decades, promising cheaper and more efficient space travel.

The idea involves a cable anchored to Earth, extending into orbit, with climbers ferrying payloads along its length. Materials like carbon nanotubes or graphene could theoretically provide the strength needed, though current technology isn't quite there yet.

If realized, a space elevator could revolutionize space exploration, making Mars colonies and lunar vacations more achievable. For now, though, it's a lofty dream—pun absolutely intended.

The Evolution of CRISPR Gene Editing

CRISPR, which stands for "Clustered Regularly Interspaced Short Palindromic Repeats," sounds like a futuristic sandwich press, but it's actually a groundbreaking tool for gene editing. Discovered in bacteria, CRISPR acts like molecular scissors, allowing scientists to snip out undesirable sections of DNA and replace them with desired sequences. Think of it as the autocorrect of genetics—only hopefully less prone to hilarious errors.

The implications are enormous. With CRISPR, we could potentially cure genetic diseases like sickle cell anemia or even prevent inherited disorders before they occur. It's also being used to develop disease-resistant crops and even explore possibilities for "designer babies" (cue ethical debates galore).

CRISPR is an incredible step forward, but with great power comes great responsibility. Editing DNA isn't something to take lightly, but it's hard not to marvel at a tool that gives us the ability to rewrite the book of life itself.

The Self-Healing Concrete

Concrete has been holding up our buildings, bridges, and egos for centuries, but it's not invincible. Enter self-healing concrete, a miraculous material infused with bacteria that spring into action when cracks form. These bacteria produce limestone when exposed to moisture, effectively sealing the crack like a biological band-aid.

The benefits are huge—fewer repairs, longer-lasting structures, and a solution to crumbling infrastructure worldwide. Plus, there's something delightfully sci-fi about buildings that can repair themselves.

Who knew the future of construction lay in harnessing nature's tiniest helpers? It's concrete innovation—literally.

The Ocean Cleanup Drone Fleet

Our oceans are drowning in plastic, but a fleet of autonomous cleanup drones is here to help. These high-tech devices are like Roombas for the sea, skimming the water's surface to collect plastic waste efficiently and sustainably.

The Ocean Cleanup project, spearheaded by Boyan Slat, aims to remove 90% of ocean plastic by 2040. The drones are solar-powered, making them eco-friendly, and are already hard at work in polluted areas like the Great Pacific Garbage Patch.

It's a hopeful reminder that technology and nature don't have to be at odds—and that a cleaner ocean starts with innovative ideas.

The Holographic Concert Experience

Imagine attending a concert where a long-deceased legend performs live on stage. Holographic technology makes this possible, creating virtual versions of artists like Tupac, Whitney Houston, and Elvis Presley. It's like time travel meets a rock show.

These performances use advanced projections and motion-capture technology to bring artists to life with startling realism.

While some find it thrilling, others argue it's a bit eerie—like a Black Mirror episode you didn't sign up for.

Love it or hate it, holographic concerts are a testament to how far tech has come in blurring the lines between reality and illusion.

The Smart Cities of Tomorrow

Imagine a city where trash bins notify collectors when they're full, traffic lights adjust to real-time conditions, and energy is distributed based on usage patterns. These are the smart cities of tomorrow, where sensors and AI optimize urban living.

Cities like Singapore and Barcelona are already leading the charge, using technology to reduce waste, improve public transportation, and make urban areas more sustainable. But smart cities aren't just about efficiency—they're about improving quality of life.

As sensors and AI become more integrated, smart cities promise a future where technology doesn't just coexist with humanity but enhances it. Here's to a cleaner, greener, and smarter tomorrow.

Geological Curiosities

The Sailing Stones of Death Valley

Death Valley, one of the hottest, driest places on Earth, seems an unlikely venue for a geological mystery. Yet its Racetrack Playa, a flat, cracked lakebed, is home to the sailing stones—rocks that inexplicably move across the desert floor, leaving long, meandering trails behind them. These stones, some weighing hundreds of pounds, have baffled scientists and sparked theories ranging from alien pranks to magnetic forces.

For decades, the phenomenon remained an enigma because no one had ever witnessed the rocks in motion. Then, in 2014, researchers armed with time-lapse cameras cracked the case. It turns out that under rare conditions, a thin layer of ice forms overnight on the playa. When the ice begins to melt, and a light wind blows, the rocks are nudged along, leaving their curious trails. It's not magic—it's physics, albeit the kind that seems too improbable for a place like Death Valley.

Though the mystery has been solved, the sailing stones still capture the imagination. They remind us that even in the harshest environments, Earth can surprise us with its slow, deliberate artistry. So if you find yourself in Death Valley, keep an eye on the playa. You might just catch a rock in motion, proving once again that even the most stubborn objects can move under the right conditions.

Krakatoa and the Loudest Sound on Earth

When Krakatoa erupted in 1883, it didn't just blow its top—it rewrote the record books. Located in the Sunda Strait between Java and Sumatra, the volcano unleashed an explosion so powerful it was heard 3,000 miles away. To put that in perspective, people in Australia thought it was cannon fire. Closer to the epicenter, eardrums burst, and tidal waves as tall as skyscrapers obliterated entire villages.

The eruption spewed so much ash and gas into the atmosphere that global temperatures dropped, and sunsets around the world turned surreal shades of orange and red. The event even inspired artistic works, with Edvard Munch's The Scream rumored to have drawn its fiery sky from Krakatoa's aftermath. In terms of geological impact, the eruption created a new volcanic island, Anak Krakatau ("Child of Krakatoa"), which continues to grow and erupt to this day.

Krakatoa serves as a dramatic reminder of the Earth's immense power. It's not every day that a single event can reshape geography, alter global weather, and still be the loudest noise in recorded history. If you ever think your neighbor's lawnmower is loud, just remember—at least it's not Krakatoa.

The Giant's Causeway in Northern Ireland

The Giant's Causeway is what happens when geology gets poetic. Located along the rugged Antrim coast, this natural wonder is made up of about 40,000 interlocking basalt columns, most of them hexagonal and so perfectly shaped they look hand-carved. According to Irish legend, the columns are the handiwork of the giant Finn McCool, who built them as a pathway to Scotland for a showdown with a rival giant.

Science, of course, offers a less mythical but equally fascinating explanation. Around 60 million years ago, volcanic activity spewed molten basalt across the landscape. As the lava cooled, it contracted and cracked, forming the polygonal shapes we see today. The result is a geological masterpiece that looks like a set piece from a fantasy epic.

Visitors can walk along the columns, marveling at the symmetry and wondering how something so ordered could arise from chaos. Whether you prefer the legend of Finn McCool or the scientific backstory, the Giant's Causeway proves that sometimes, nature itself is the greatest sculptor.

The Devil's Kettle Waterfall

In Judge C.R. Magney State Park, Minnesota, lies a waterfall with a split personality. Known as the Devil's Kettle, this geological oddity is a two-tiered waterfall where one half flows into the river below, while the other half plunges into a mysterious hole and seemingly vanishes. Where does the water go? That's been the million-dollar question for decades.

People have tried throwing everything from dye to ping-pong balls into the hole, hoping to trace its path, but nothing ever reappears downstream. For a while, theories ranged from underground caves to supernatural portals. After all, with a name like "Devil's Kettle," you'd expect a little drama.

Recent research suggests the disappearing water doesn't go far—it likely seeps through cracks in the rock and rejoins the river underground. But even with this explanation, the Devil's Kettle retains its allure. There's something captivating about a natural feature that seems to defy logic, inviting us to question what lies beneath the surface. It's a reminder that even in the age of Google Earth and high-tech mapping, some of nature's mysteries remain tantalizingly unsolved.

Blue Lava at Kawah Ijen Volcano, Indonesia

Volcanoes are typically associated with fiery reds and oranges, but Kawah Ijen in Indonesia adds a surreal twist to the volcanic palette. By night, this sulfur-rich volcano dazzles with glowing blue flames, an eerie spectacle that looks like it belongs in a sci-fi movie. However, this "blue lava" isn't lava at all. The phenomenon occurs when sulfuric gases escape from cracks in the volcano, ignite upon contact with oxygen, and burn in brilliant electric blue.

The glow is most visible in the dark, attracting adventurers and photographers willing to brave the hike and the pungent smell of sulfur. But Kawah Ijen isn't just a visual marvel; it's also home to a harsh yet industrious reality. Local miners harvest sulfur from the crater, carrying heavy loads of the bright yellow mineral down treacherous paths. The contrast between the beauty of the blue flames and the grueling work of the miners creates a striking juxtaposition.

Kawah Ijen is a vivid reminder of nature's creativity and unpredictability. It's as if the Earth decided it was tired of regular fire and wanted to experiment with something new. But don't let the Instagram-worthy glow fool you—this beauty comes with a side of danger, as the toxic gases are no joke for those who linger too long.

The Singing Sand Dunes

Who knew sand could carry a tune? In certain deserts around the world, sand dunes have been known to "sing," producing eerie, musical tones that range from a low hum to a deep roar. This natural orchestra is caused by grains of sand rubbing together under the right conditions—typically dry weather and a specific grain size. The sound is often compared to a distant airplane or a reverberating bass note, but unlike your karaoke skills, this singing is entirely pitch-perfect.

One of the best places to hear this phenomenon is in the Sahara Desert, but singing dunes can also be found in China, the United States, and even Wales. The exact mechanism behind the sound has puzzled scientists for centuries, though modern research suggests that the vibrations occur when sand grains slide down the slope of a dune, creating resonant frequencies.

The "songs" of the dunes have inspired myths and legends among local populations. In some cultures, the sounds were thought to be the whispers of spirits or warnings from the gods. Today, they serve as both a geological curiosity and a quirky reminder that even sand has its moments of artistry.

The Darvaza Gas Crater (The Door to Hell)

If Hell had a front porch, it would probably look like the Darvaza Gas Crater in Turkmenistan. This fiery pit, aptly nicknamed the "Door to Hell," has been burning continuously for more than 50 years. The crater, about 230 feet wide, was accidentally created in 1971 when Soviet geologists were drilling for natural gas. The ground collapsed, exposing a massive underground cavern filled with gas. In an attempt to prevent toxic fumes from spreading, the geologists set the gas on fire, assuming it would burn off in a few days. Spoiler alert: it didn't.

The result is a perpetually burning inferno that looks like something out of Dante's Inferno. The flames illuminate the desert night, drawing adventurous tourists despite its remote location. Standing at the edge of the crater, you can feel the heat and hear the roar of the fire—a visceral reminder of the Earth's untamed power.

While the crater is an environmental oddity, it has also become a strange symbol of resilience. Turkmenistan has even considered closing it to reduce its ecological impact, but for now, the Door to Hell continues to mesmerize anyone brave enough to visit. Just don't bring marshmallows—this bonfire is strictly for looking, not roasting.

The Moeraki Boulders in New Zealand

Along the windswept beaches of New Zealand's Otago coast, you'll find the Moeraki Boulders—giant, perfectly spherical rocks scattered like forgotten marbles from a game played by giants. These geological wonders are not man-made but rather the result of a natural process called concretion, where mineral deposits gradually form around a core over millions of years, like a pearl in an oyster.

Some of the boulders are small enough to sit on, while others are over six feet in diameter, making them the perfect backdrop for dramatic selfies. Maori legend, however, offers a more poetic explanation: the boulders are the remains of gourds and eel baskets washed ashore from the wreck of an ancestral canoe. The blend of scientific and mythical interpretations adds to their charm.

Over time, erosion has exposed these spherical wonders, creating a surreal landscape that looks like the remnants of a lost civilization. Tourists flock to the site to marvel at their symmetry and speculate about their origins. Whether you see them as nature's bowling balls or relics of ancient myths, the Moeraki Boulders are a testament to the Earth's ability to shape something so perfectly out of chaos.

The Richat Structure (Eye of the Sahara)

If the Sahara Desert had a bullseye, it would be the Richat Structure, a massive circular formation so striking it's nicknamed the "Eye of the Sahara." Visible from space, this geological oddity spans nearly 30 miles and has puzzled scientists and adventurers alike. From above, it looks like an ancient crater left behind by an enormous asteroid. But despite appearances, there's no evidence that an asteroid had anything to do with it.

Geologists believe the Richat Structure is a deeply eroded geological dome, with concentric rings formed by the uplifting and subsequent weathering of different rock layers. Think of it as Earth's version of a layer cake—only this one is made of sandstone, igneous rock, and ancient mystery. Still, its perfect symmetry invites speculation. Some say it's the remains of the lost city of Atlantis, though no credible evidence supports that claim.

Whether you believe in geological forces or mythical origins, the Richat Structure is undeniably captivating. Its size and symmetry make it a favorite among astronauts who often photograph it from space. Down on Earth, it's less dramatic—a vast, rocky expanse surrounded by endless desert. Yet, it remains a reminder that even in the most barren landscapes, Earth holds surprises waiting to be unearthed.

The Chocolate Hills of Bohol, Philippines

The Chocolate Hills of Bohol are a sweet tooth's dream—if only they were edible. This surreal landscape consists of more than 1,200 conical hills that turn a rich chocolate brown during the dry season, creating a scene that looks like something out of Charlie and the Chocolate Factory. But while they might resemble candy, their origin is entirely geological.

The hills are made of limestone covered in grass. Over thousands of years, rain and erosion sculpted the terrain into these symmetrical mounds, giving them their unique shape. Local legends, however, offer more colorful explanations. One story tells of two feuding giants who hurled boulders at each other, only to leave behind their mess when they reconciled. Another tale speaks of a lovesick giant who wept for his unrequited love, his tears hardening into hills.

Whatever their origin, the Chocolate Hills are a UNESCO-listed wonder and a major tourist attraction. Visitors can climb viewpoints to marvel at the natural symmetry and snap photos that could fool anyone into believing they've stumbled upon the world's largest box of chocolates. But beware—if you visit during the wet season, the hills are a lush green, a stunning transformation but decidedly less "chocolatey."

Fairy Chimneys of Cappadocia, Turkey

Cappadocia's Fairy Chimneys are what happens when nature and history collide in a spectacularly whimsical way. These towering rock formations, carved by centuries of wind and volcanic eruptions, rise from the Turkish landscape like something straight out of a fantasy novel. Their bulbous tops and slender bases give them the appearance of oversized mushrooms—or, as the name suggests, homes for fairies.

The real magic of the Fairy Chimneys lies in their human connection. Over the centuries, locals carved homes, churches, and even monasteries into the soft volcanic tuff, creating entire underground cities. These spaces weren't just for show—they served as refuges during invasions, offering shelter and secret passageways. Some of the ancient frescoes in the rock-hewn churches still survive, adding a layer of artistry to this geological wonder.

Today, the Fairy Chimneys are a must-see destination, drawing visitors who marvel at the interplay of natural beauty and human ingenuity. Whether you're exploring the ancient dwellings or taking a hot air balloon ride to view them from above, Cappadocia offers a landscape unlike anywhere else on Earth. It's a place where nature sculpts, history engraves, and your imagination soars.

The Crystal Cave of Giants in Mexico

Imagine stepping into a world straight out of Superman's Fortress of Solitude, but instead of Krypton, you're in Mexico. The Crystal Cave of Giants, located beneath the Naica Mine, is home to some of the largest crystals ever discovered. These towering selenite formations stretch over 30 feet long and weigh several tons, making them look more like frozen lightning bolts than mineral deposits. It's a geological masterpiece created over hundreds of thousands of years, thanks to the cave's unique conditions: high temperatures and mineral-rich groundwater.

But visiting this sparkling wonderland isn't for the faint of heart — or the ill-prepared. The cave's intense heat (up to 136°F) and humidity can make exploring it feel like trekking through a sauna on steroids. Scientists and adventurers need specialized cooling suits and limited exposure time to avoid overheating. Despite these challenges, the Crystal Cave has offered unparalleled insights into the growth of crystals and the ancient environment that fostered them.

Sadly, the cave is now mostly flooded, making access even more difficult. Yet, its brief moment of discovery in the early 2000s revealed one of Earth's most dazzling secrets. It's a reminder that even in the depths of the Earth, nature has a knack for creating beauty on a monumental scale.

Earthquake Lights

Imagine seeing the sky light up with eerie flashes of green, blue, or white just before the ground starts shaking. No, it's not an alien invasion or a preview of the apocalypse — it's earthquake lights, one of nature's strangest and least understood phenomena. These mysterious illuminations have been reported for centuries, yet scientists are still scratching their heads over how they happen.

Theories abound. Some suggest that the lights are caused by electrical charges released from stressed rocks along fault lines. Others point to piezoelectric effects — certain rocks generating electrical currents when compressed. Still, the exact mechanism remains elusive, and the phenomenon doesn't occur with every earthquake, adding another layer of mystery.

What makes earthquake lights so fascinating is their unpredictability. They've been reported before major quakes, during the shaking, and even afterward, making them an unreliable warning system. However, they are consistent in one thing: their ability to freak people out. Witnesses describe glowing orbs, streaks of light, or flashes resembling lightning, all set against an already terrifying backdrop of trembling Earth.

Whether they're nature's way of adding theatrics to an already dramatic event or a genuine precursor to seismic activity, earthquake lights continue to intrigue both scientists and skywatchers. For now, they remain one of Earth's most dazzling unsolved mysteries.

The Great Blue Hole of Belize

The Great Blue Hole of Belize is the kind of place that makes you wonder if the ocean is hiding secrets from us. This giant marine sinkhole, over 1,000 feet wide and 400 feet deep, is a diver's dream and a geologist's delight. Located near the center of Lighthouse Reef, the hole's perfectly circular shape and deep blue hue make it look like a portal to another world — or at least to Atlantis.

The sinkhole was formed thousands of years ago during the Ice Age when rising sea levels flooded a massive limestone cavern, causing its roof to collapse. What's left is a natural wonder filled with stalactites, stalagmites, and an otherworldly sense of calm. Divers flock here to explore its depths, encountering everything from reef sharks to strange formations that seem to defy gravity.

Jacques Cousteau famously declared the Great Blue Hole one of the top diving sites in the world, and it's easy to see why. But even for those who prefer to stay dry, the hole's sheer scale and beauty are awe-inspiring. Whether you see it as a geological marvel or a spooky reminder of Earth's hidden forces, the Great Blue Hole is proof that sometimes, the most mysterious places are right beneath our feet — or in this case, beneath the waves.

The Stone Forest of Madagascar

Madagascar's Stone Forest, or Tsingy, isn't your average forest — it's more like nature's version of an obstacle course. This labyrinth of jagged limestone formations rises sharply from the Earth, creating a maze of towering spires that look more like sculptures than rocks. The name "Tsingy" translates to "where one cannot walk barefoot," which is both an apt description and a polite warning.

Formed over millions of years by water eroding the limestone, the Tsingy is a testament to the patient artistry of nature. Its dramatic peaks and crevices house an astonishing array of biodiversity, including species found nowhere else on Earth. Lemurs, rare reptiles, and even tiny frogs make their homes among the spiky formations, proving that even the harshest landscapes can support life.

Exploring the Tsingy isn't for the faint of heart — or the clumsy. Visitors traverse narrow bridges, climb steep rock faces, and squeeze through tight passages, all while marveling at the surreal beauty of the terrain. Despite its ruggedness, the Stone Forest is a UNESCO World Heritage Site and a must-see for adventurous travelers.

The Tsingy is more than just a geological curiosity; it's a living, breathing ecosystem and a natural wonder that combines danger and beauty in equal measure. It's proof that even in the remotest corners of the Earth, nature is always at its most creative.

The Blood Falls of Antarctica

In the frozen silence of Antarctica, there's a sight that seems more at home in a vampire movie than on Earth. The Blood Falls, a bright red cascade spilling from the Taylor Glacier, looks like nature's version of a horror show. But there's no need to call Buffy — this phenomenon is all about geology, not the undead. The eerie red color comes from iron-rich water that has been trapped beneath the glacier for millions of years. As the water emerges and reacts with oxygen, the iron oxidizes, turning a deep, rusty red, much like liquid iron spilling from the planet's veins.

The origin of this otherworldly waterfall is just as fascinating as its appearance. Scientists believe the water source is a subglacial lake cut off from the surface for millennia. This isolated ecosystem contains microbes that have survived in complete darkness without oxygen, relying on iron and sulfur to fuel their existence. Essentially, Blood Falls is both a geological wonder and a time capsule for ancient microbial life.

Its discovery challenges our understanding of life in extreme conditions, making it a hot topic (well, as hot as Antarctica gets) for astrobiologists looking for clues about potential life on other icy planets or moons. Blood Falls might look like a crime scene, but it's a masterpiece of Earth's adaptability, proving that even in the coldest corners of the world, life — and drama — finds a way.

The Magnetic Hill Mystery

Imagine this: you park your car at the base of a hill, put it in neutral, and then watch in awe as it appears to roll uphill all on its own. Welcome to Magnetic Hill, where gravity seems to take a day off, and logic gets turned upside down. Found in various locations around the world, these hills are the stuff of roadside attraction legends, luring visitors to experience the "magic" firsthand.

The truth behind Magnetic Hill is less supernatural and more optical illusion. The surrounding landscape creates a perspective trick that makes a slight downhill slope appear as if it's going uphill. Trees, fences, and the horizon all conspire to play a game of visual deception. But even when you know the science, the effect is still delightfully mind-bending.

These spots have inspired a fair share of folklore. Some claim the phenomenon is caused by magnetic forces in the Earth, while others weave tales of ghostly interference or alien experiments. In reality, it's a reminder that our senses can't always be trusted, and a well-placed hill can outsmart even the most skeptical among us. Magnetic Hills aren't just quirky; they're a humbling testament to the power of perception.

The Singing Icebergs

Antarctica is home to many wonders, but few are as haunting as its singing icebergs. These enormous ice structures aren't just picturesque — they're vocal, emitting eerie, low-frequency sounds that travel for miles. The tones are so otherworldly that you'd be forgiven for thinking the icebergs are whispering secrets about their ancient origins — or maybe plotting something sinister.

The "songs" are caused by vibrations within the iceberg as it interacts with surrounding water. When winds or currents move the ice, it resonates, producing sounds that range from a ghostly hum to deep rumbles reminiscent of whale calls. Scientists studying these sounds have even likened them to musical instruments, albeit ones made entirely of frozen water.

But these icy serenades aren't just for show. They provide valuable information about iceberg stability, water currents, and climate conditions. Listening to an iceberg sing is like eavesdropping on nature's data logs — if you can decipher the tune, that is. While the sounds may be haunting, they also highlight the beauty of our planet's frozen realms, where even silence isn't truly silent.

The Wave in Arizona

If you've ever wondered what it would look like if the ocean turned to stone mid-surf, look no further than The Wave in Arizona. This surreal sandstone formation, located in the Coyote Buttes North area, is a swirling masterpiece of wind and water erosion. Its wavelike patterns and rich hues of red, orange, and gold make it one of the most photographed geological wonders in the world — and one of the most sought-after hiking destinations.

The Wave was formed over millions of years as wind sculpted layers of sandstone into its current undulating shape. The effect is so striking that it looks more like a painter's palette than a natural rock formation. It's a photographer's dream and a geologist's playground, combining aesthetic beauty with scientific intrigue.

But visiting The Wave isn't as simple as showing up with a camera. Access is restricted to preserve its fragile beauty, with only a limited number of daily permits issued through a lottery system. For those lucky enough to experience it in person, The Wave offers an almost otherworldly journey through Earth's artistic side. It's a reminder that even in the dry, dusty deserts of Arizona, nature can still find ways to create something truly magical.

The Fingal's Cave of Scotland

Tucked away on the uninhabited island of Staffa in Scotland lies Fingal's Cave, a geological wonder that's as mesmerizing to the eyes as it is to the ears. This sea cave isn't just any ordinary cavern—it's a symphony of nature's design, carved from hexagonal basalt columns that look like they belong in an architect's sketchbook rather than a remote volcanic island. These towering geometric formations were created millions of years ago by cooling lava, and their near-perfect symmetry seems almost too precise to be real.

But the magic of Fingal's Cave doesn't stop at its appearance. Step inside, and you'll be greeted by acoustics so extraordinary they've earned the cave its nickname, "Nature's Cathedral." Waves crashing against the walls produce hauntingly beautiful echoes, as if the cave itself is humming along with the sea. This natural amphitheater has inspired countless artists and musicians, most famously Felix Mendelssohn. After visiting in 1829, he composed his Hebrides Overture, capturing the cave's ethereal beauty in a sweeping orchestral piece.

Legends swirl around the cave as well, with tales of giants and heroes adding a layer of folklore to its already otherworldly appeal. Whether you're drawn by its scientific intrigue, artistic legacy, or mythical aura, Fingal's Cave is a masterpiece of nature's craft. It's a place where geology meets poetry, a quiet reminder that the Earth itself can be the most profound creator of art and music.

Fun Quiz: Your Trivia Buffness

Choose the best answer for each of the following 20 questions.
At the end of the fun quiz, follow the scoring instructions to
determine your level of trivia buffness.

1. You overhear someone at a party say, "I wonder why
flamingos are pink." Do you:

A) Quietly Google the answer and share it.
B) Launch into a detailed explanation.
C) Pretend you didn't hear and grab another snack.

2. When you see a fun fact on a cereal box, you:

A) Memorize it for later.
B) Correct it if it's wrong.
C) Toss it and move on.

3. You're stuck in traffic with a trivia podcast on. Do you:

A) Listen intently and answer out loud.
B) Pause the podcast to fact-check a claim.
C) Switch to music because you're too distracted.

4. Have you ever quoted a trivia fact to win an argument?

A) Guilty as charged!
B) I'd never weaponize trivia… would I?
C) Nope, I keep my trivia and my arguments separate.

5. You find a random trivia book in a store. Do you:

A) Buy it immediately.

B) Skim through it for facts to share later.
C) Appreciate it and walk away.

6. Do you correct friends' random trivia facts if they're wrong?

A) Always.
B) Only if it's wildly inaccurate.
C) Never—I'd hate to be that person.

7. When someone asks you to name a random fact, you:

A) Spout one immediately.
B) Need a moment to decide which one to share.
C) Shrug—it's too much pressure.

8. Your idea of a dream vacation involves:

A) A trip to a museum or historical site.
B) A trivia-themed cruise.
C) Anything but trivia—vacations are for relaxing.

9. Which of these would excite you most?

A) A trivia championship.
B) A surprise fact in your favorite show.
C) A day with no questions at all.

10. Have you ever Googled "weird facts" just for fun?

A) Frequently.
B) Occasionally.
C) Never—it's not my thing.

11. Do you know your city's weirdest historical fact?

A) Yes, I tell everyone about it.

B) I think I do.
C) Nope, no clue.

12. Would you attend a trivia night alone if your friends bailed?

A) Of course!
B) I'd consider it.
C) Never — I'm not that dedicated.

13. How many trivia apps or games do you have on your phone?

A) Too many to count.
B) A couple.
C) None.

14. Do you have a favorite "go-to" trivia fact?

A) Absolutely!
B) Not really, but I know plenty.
C) Nope, who needs one?

15. Your favorite section of a trivia book is:

A) Science and nature.
B) History and culture.
C) None — I don't read trivia books.

16. You're at a quiz night, and your team names itself:

A) "Fact-tastic Four."
B) "Trivia Titans."
C) "Here for the Drinks."

17. Do you ever fact-check trivia books or quizzes?

A) Regularly.

B) Occasionally.
C) Never—who has time for that?

18. If you hear a strange fact that seems unbelievable, you:

A) Research it immediately.
B) File it away and maybe check later.
C) Forget about it—it's probably not true.

19. How do you feel about "useless trivia"?

A) There's no such thing—it's all fascinating!
B) Fun but not essential.
C) Useless trivia is redundant, right?

20. What's your goal with trivia?

A) Learn as much as possible.
B) Impress friends and family.
C) Get through trivia night without embarrassing myself.

Scoring and Results:

Mostly A's: Trivia Overlord – You reign supreme in the world of random facts. Your knowledge knows no bounds, and others tremble before your encyclopedic might.

Mostly B's: Fact Ninja – Silent but deadly with your trivia strikes, you know just enough to impress without overwhelming, striking the perfect balance of smarts and stealth.

Mostly C's: Trivia Tadpole – You're just starting to swim in the vast ocean of trivia knowledge, but every tadpole has the potential to become a trivia beast one day.